Coloring Books For Adults Vol. 4

40 Stress Relieving And Relaxing Patterns

Adult Coloring Books Series By

www.ColoringCraze.com

ISBN: 9781521172339
Edition: 4

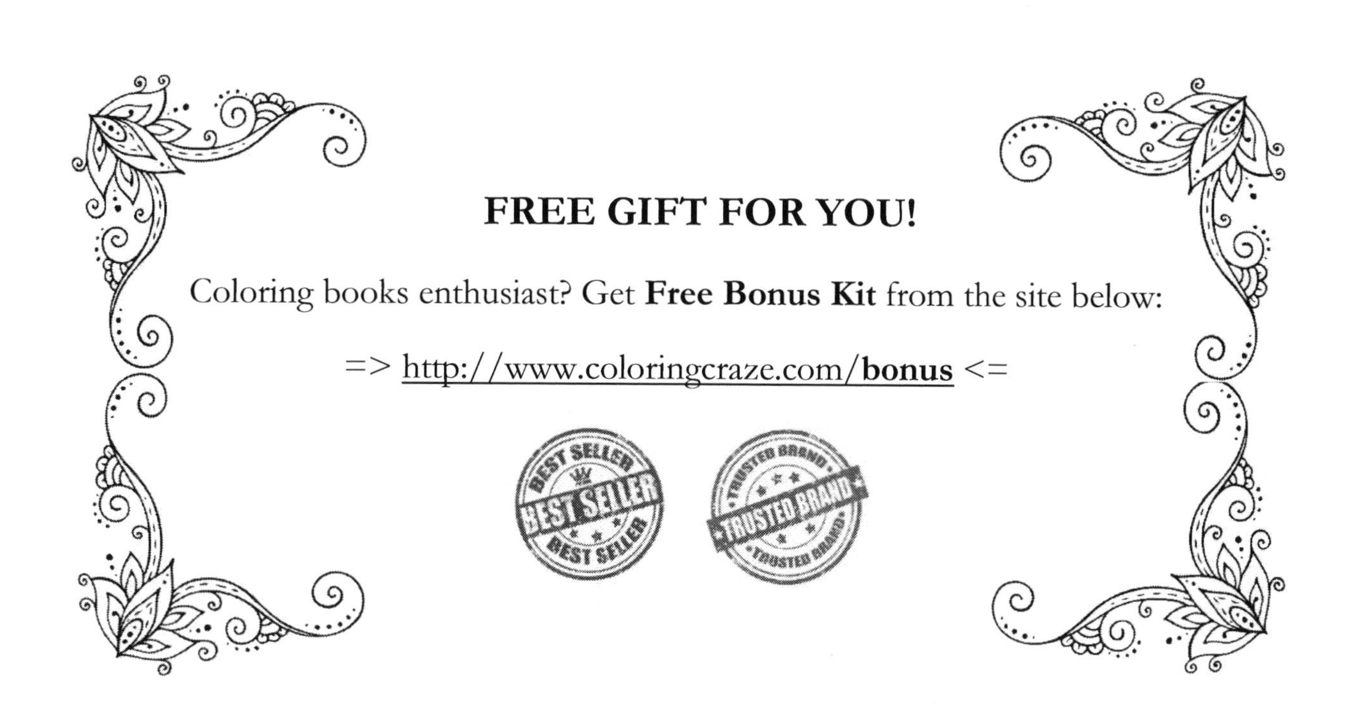

FREE GIFT FOR YOU!

Coloring books enthusiast? Get **Free Bonus Kit** from the site below:

=> http://www.coloringcraze.com/**bonus** <=

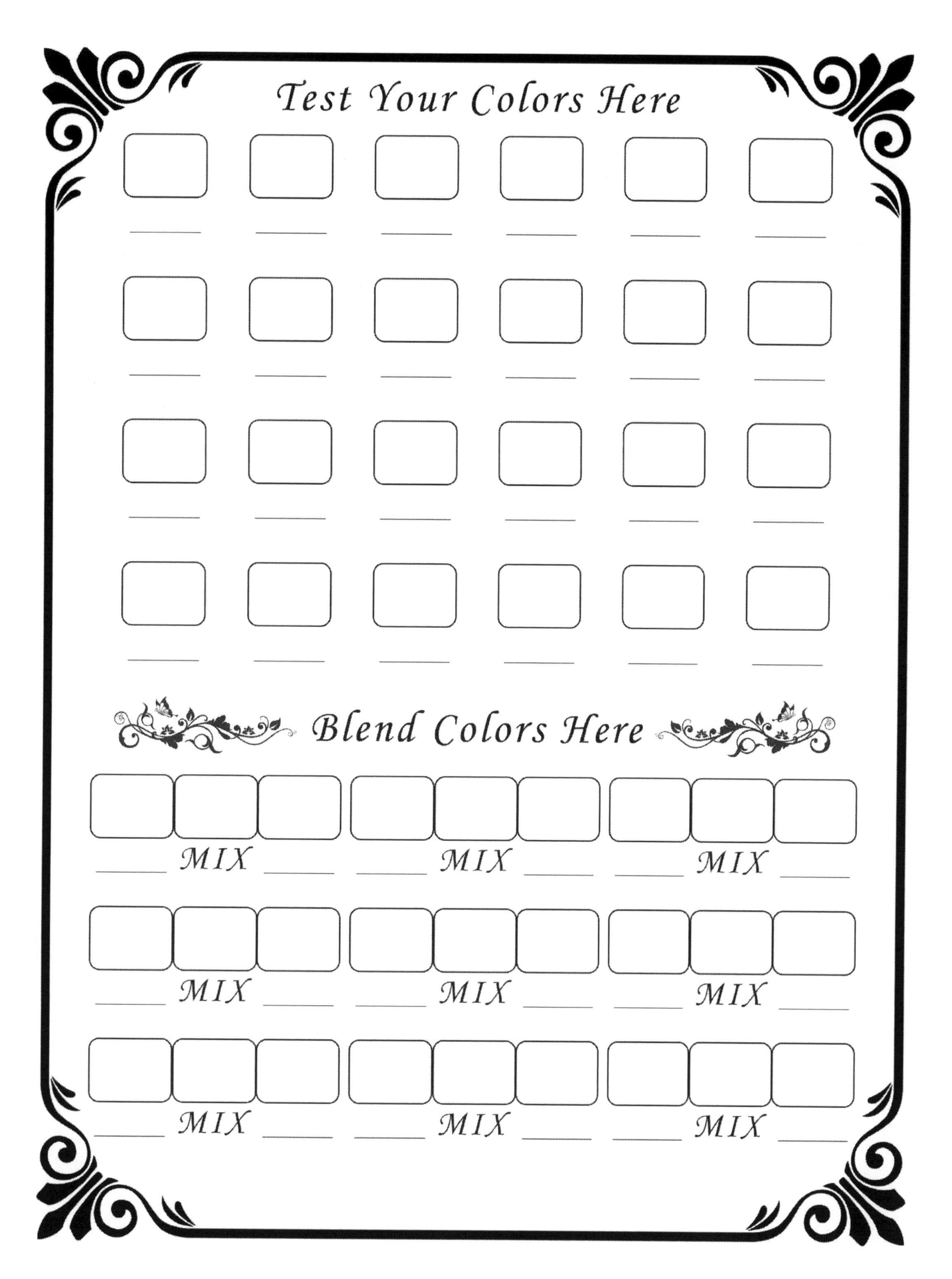
Test Your Colors Here
Blend Colors Here
MIX
MIX
MIX
MIX
MIX
MIX
MIX
MIX
MIX

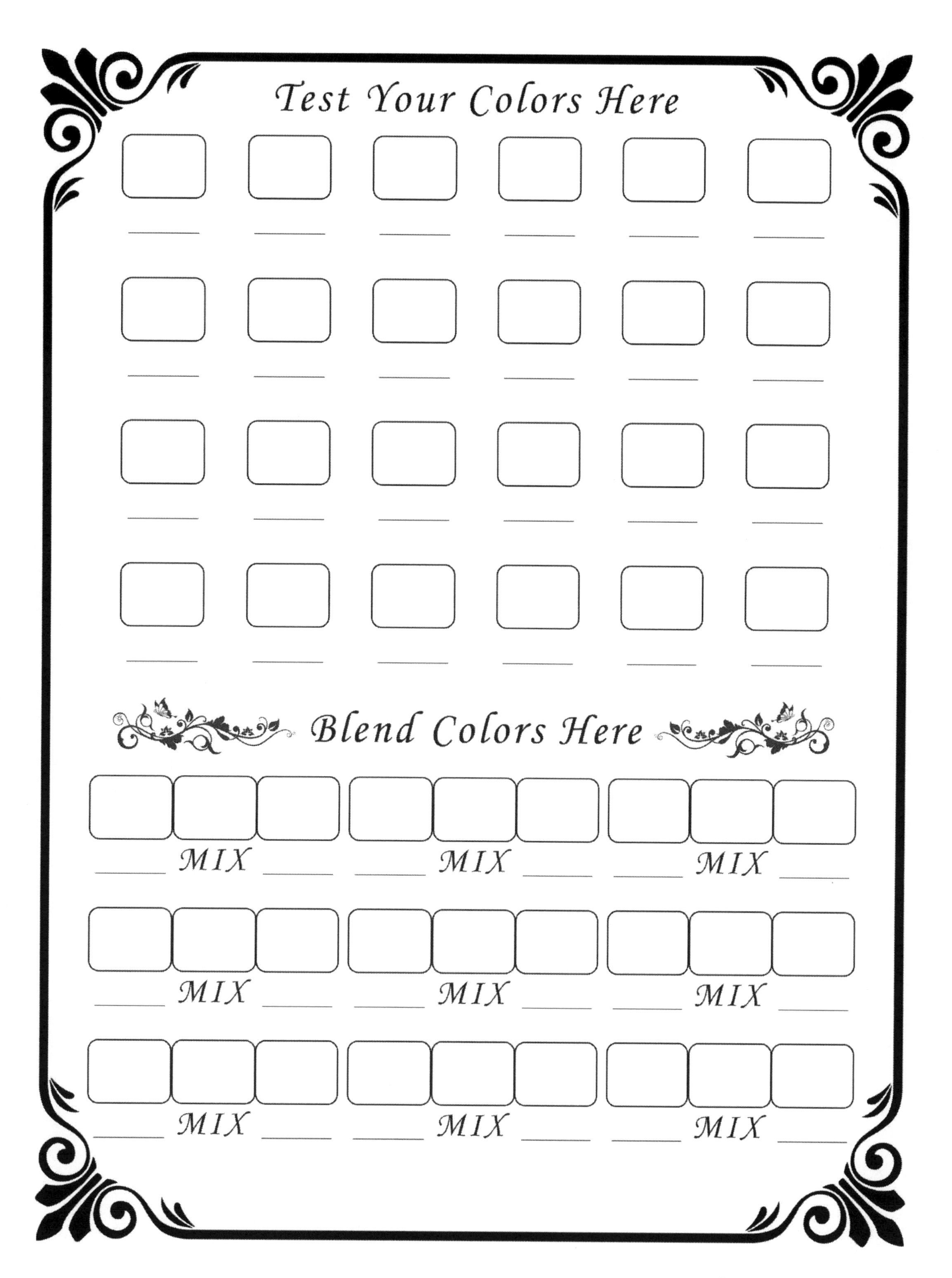
Test Your Colors Here
Blend Colors Here
MIX
MIX
MIX
MIX
MIX
MIX
MIX
MIX
MIX

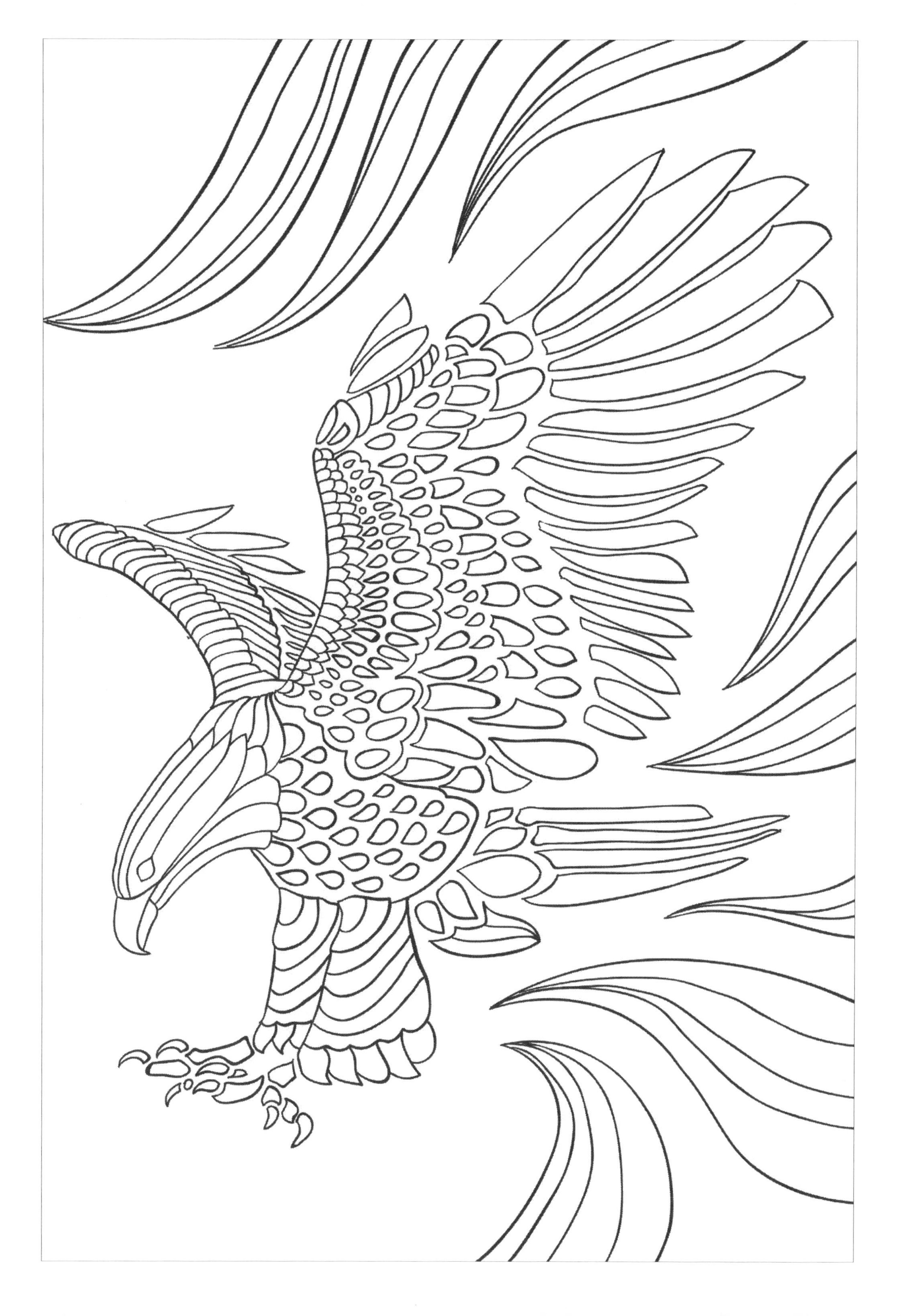

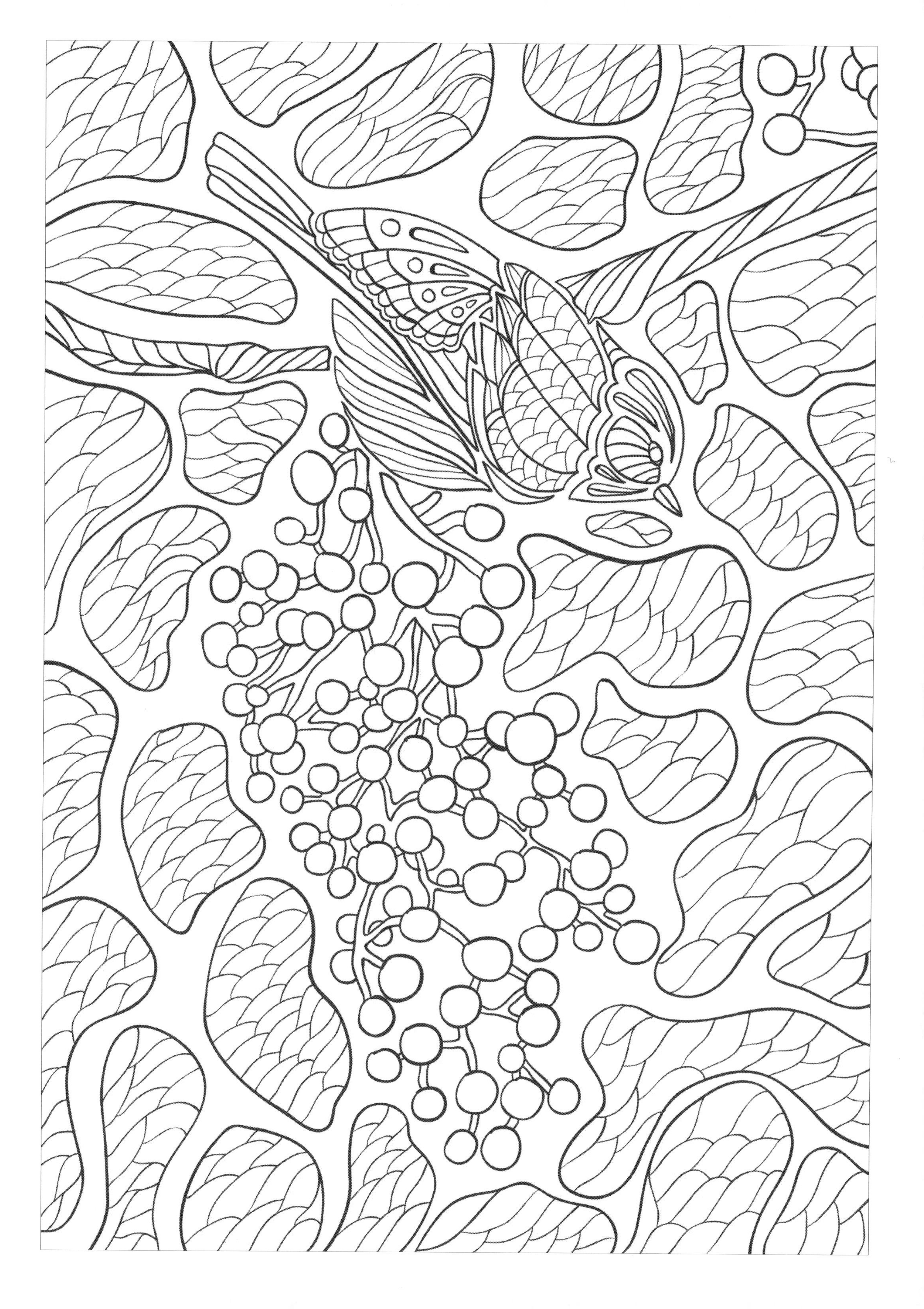

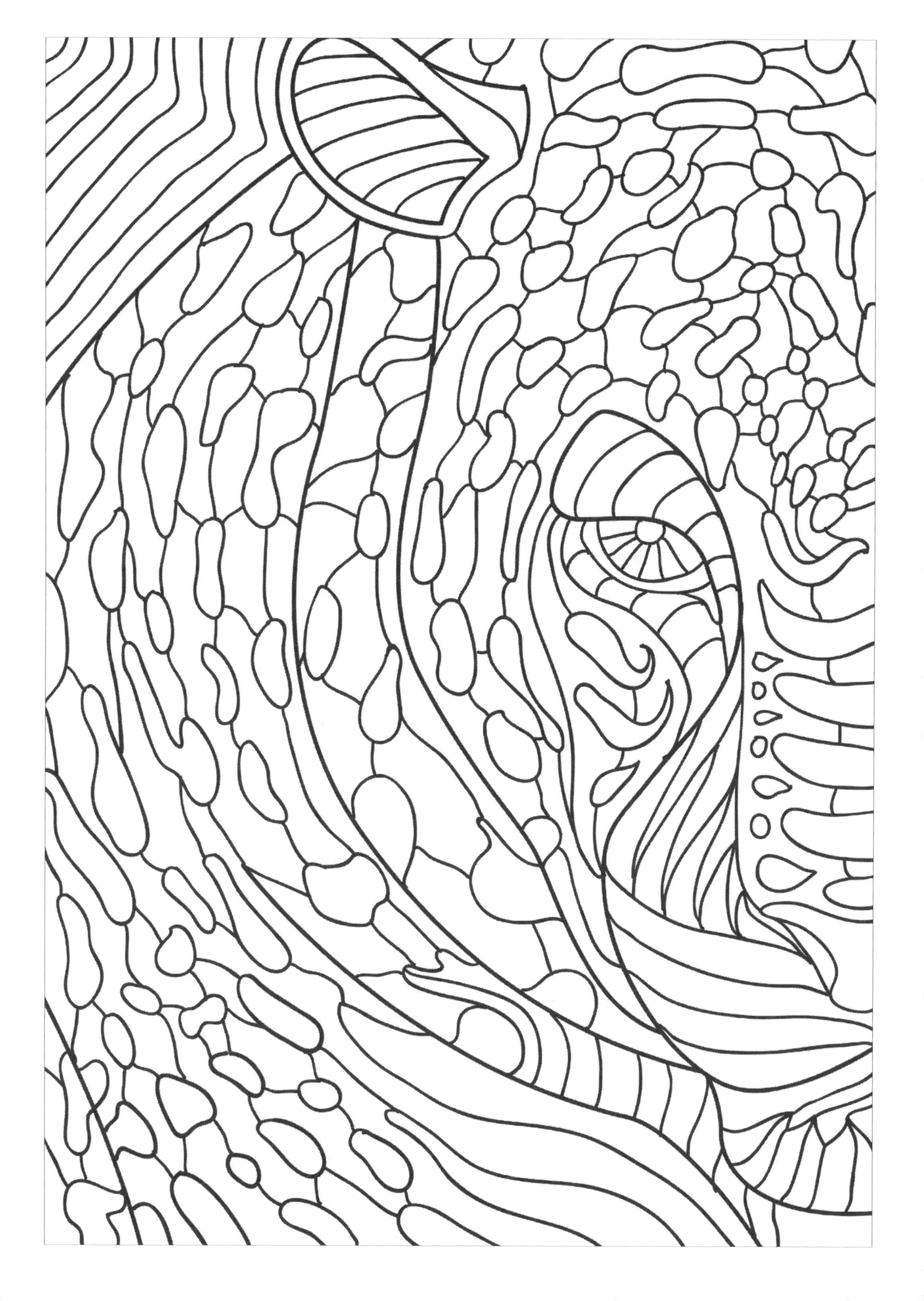

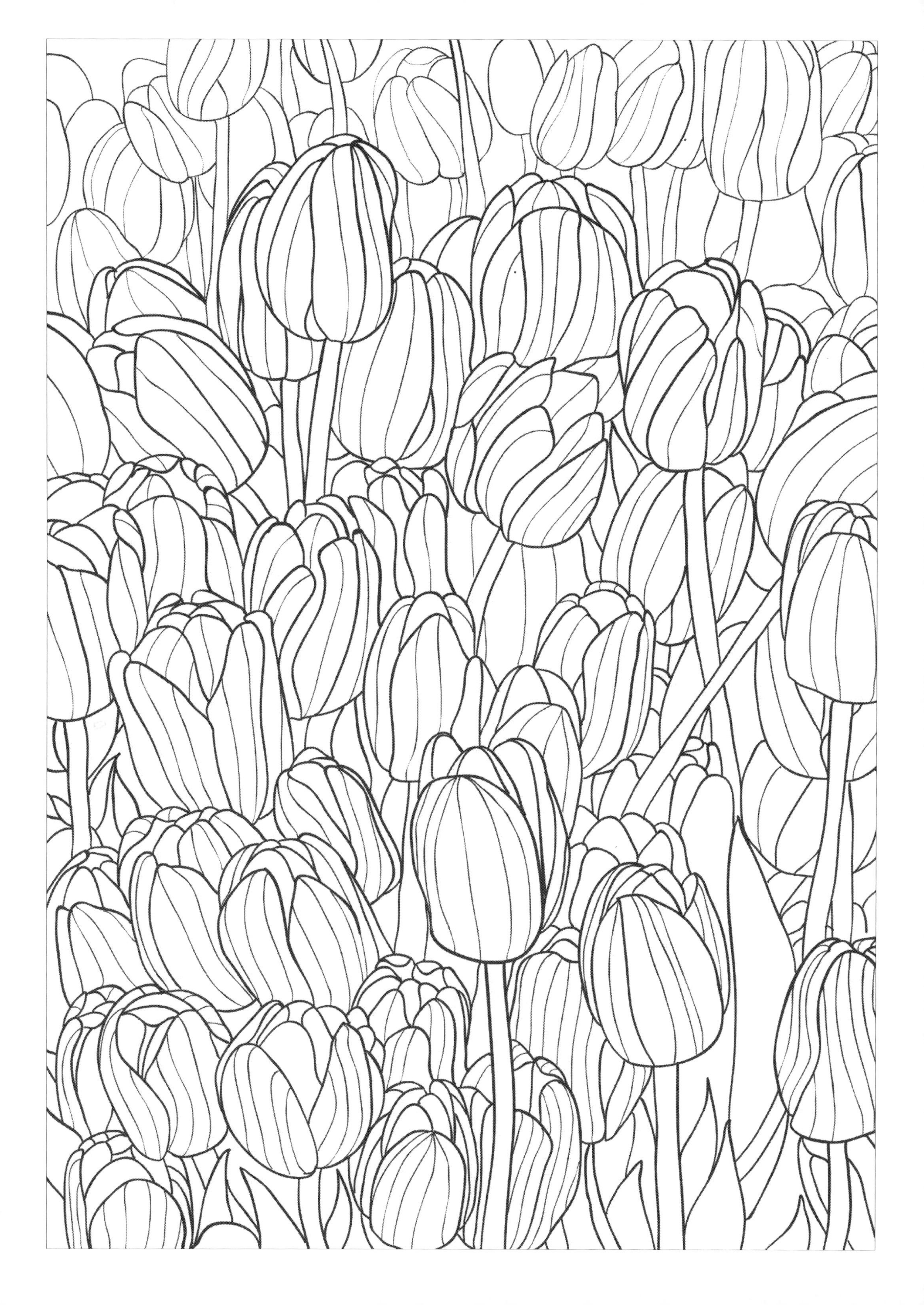

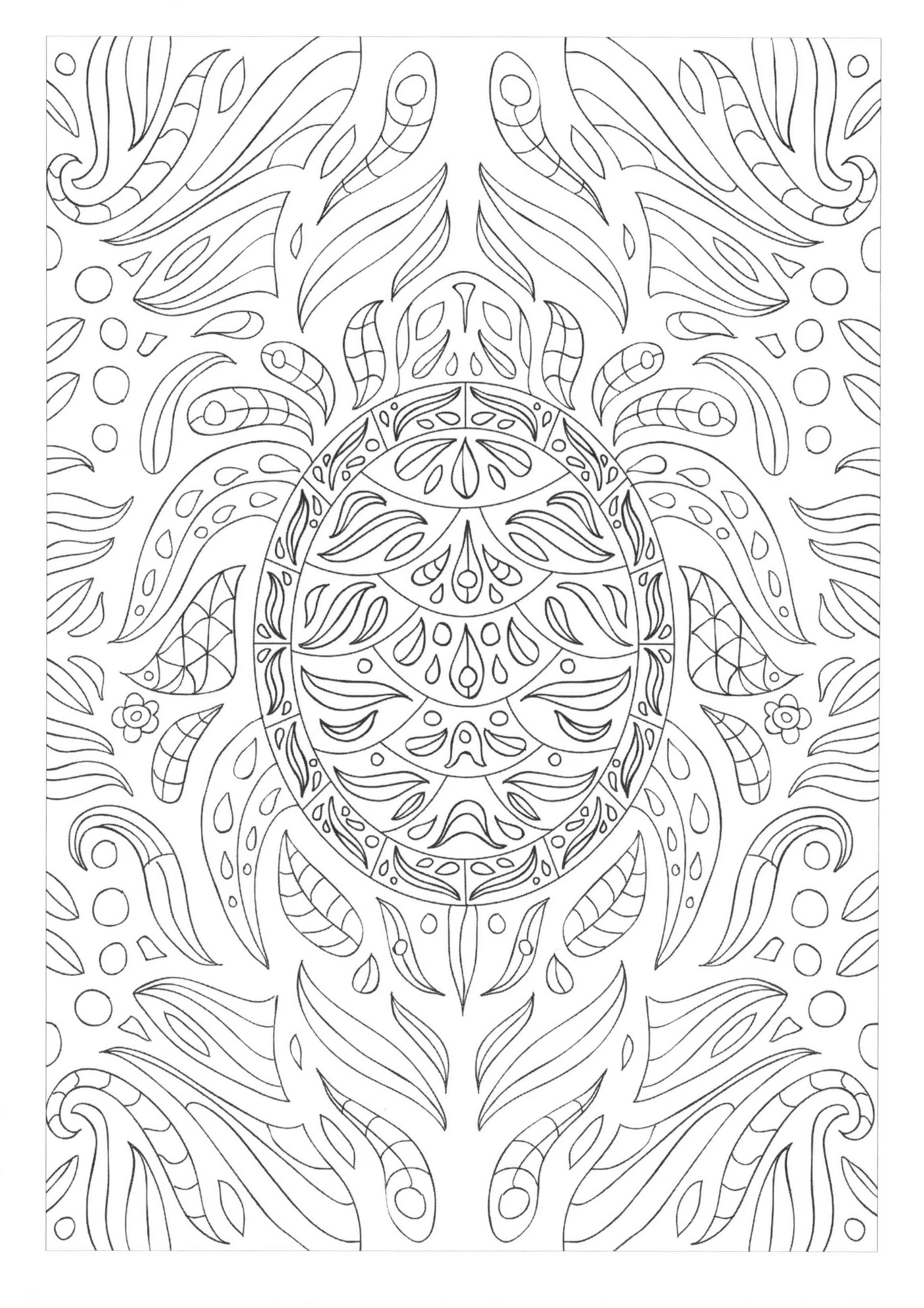

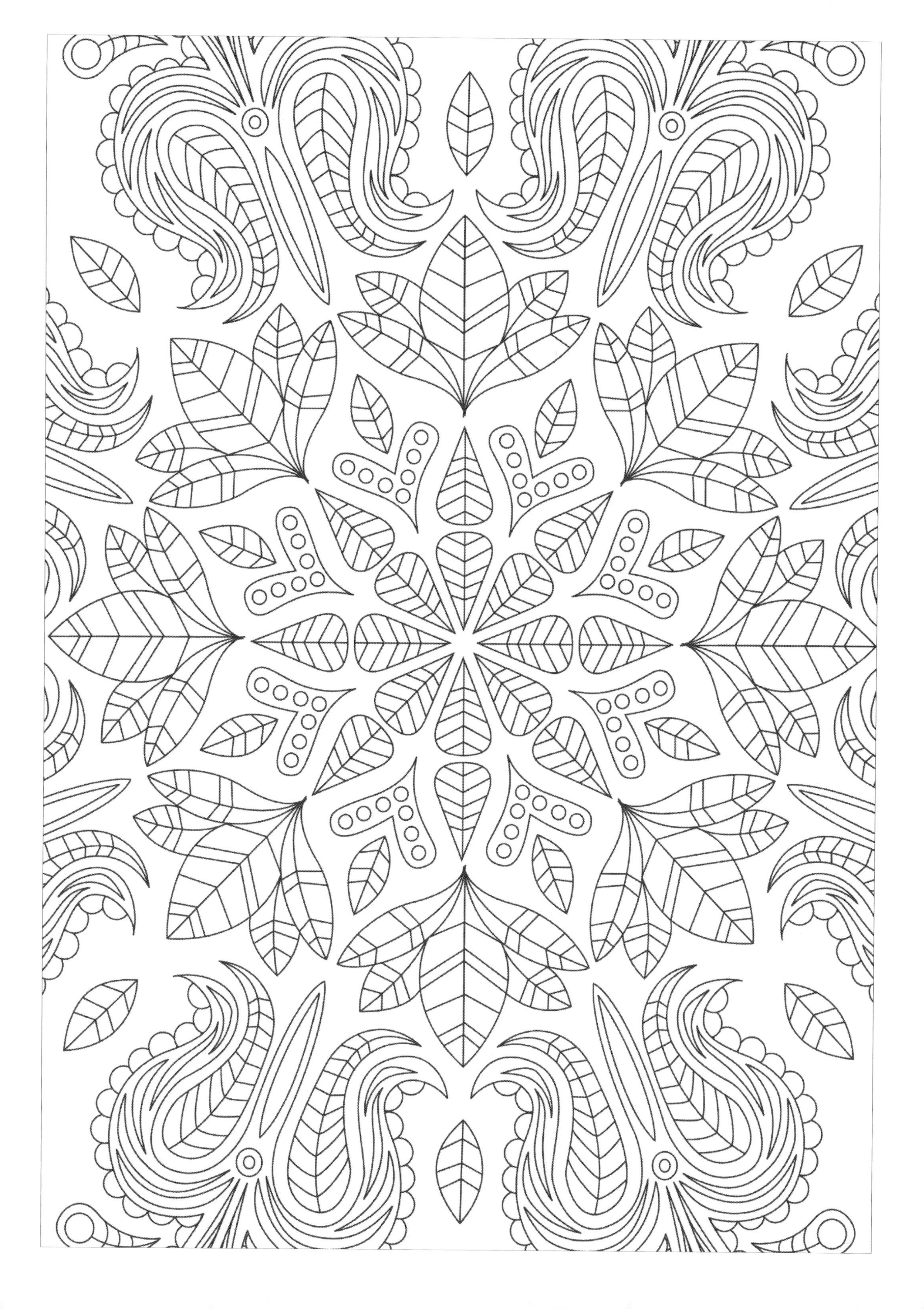

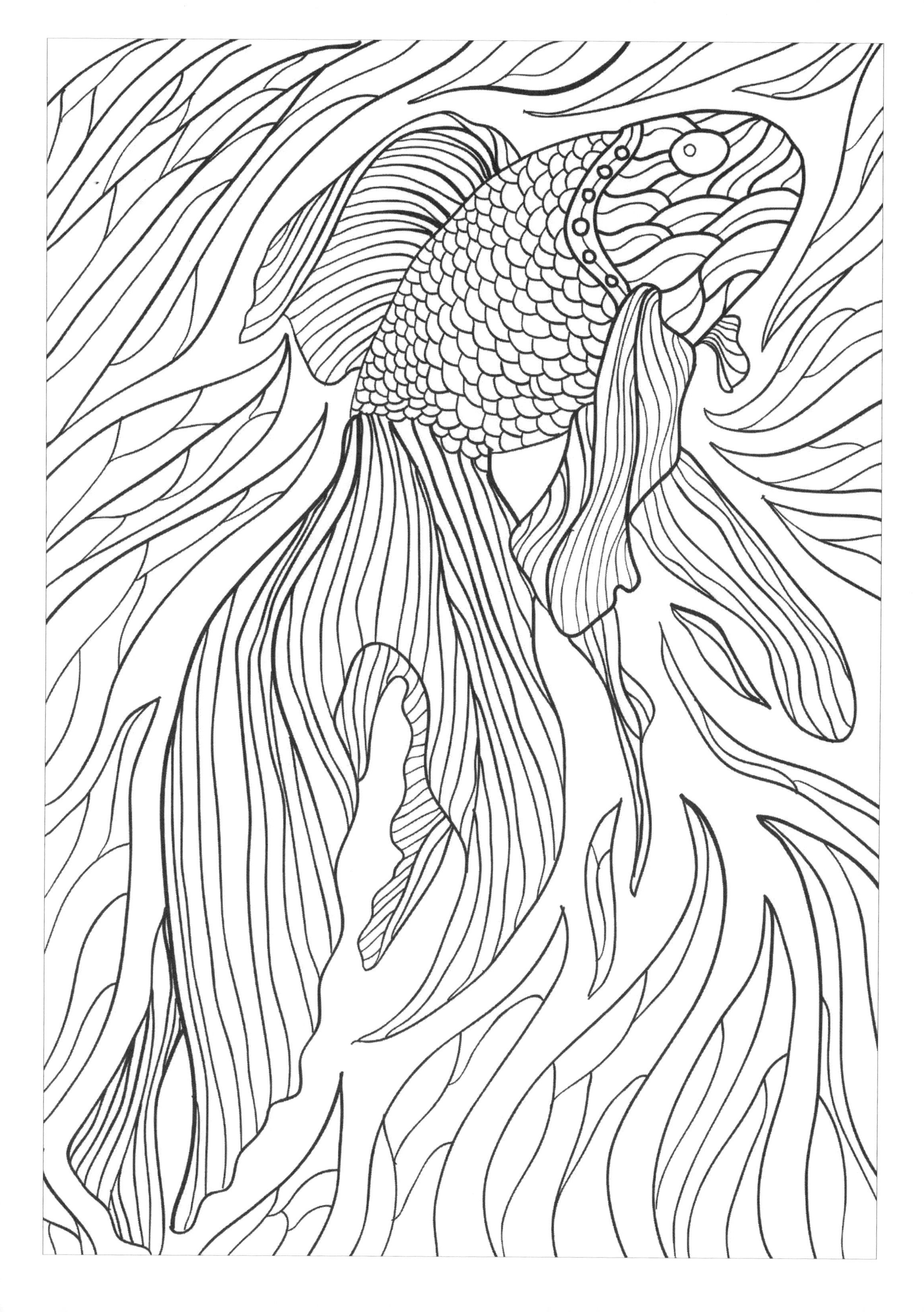

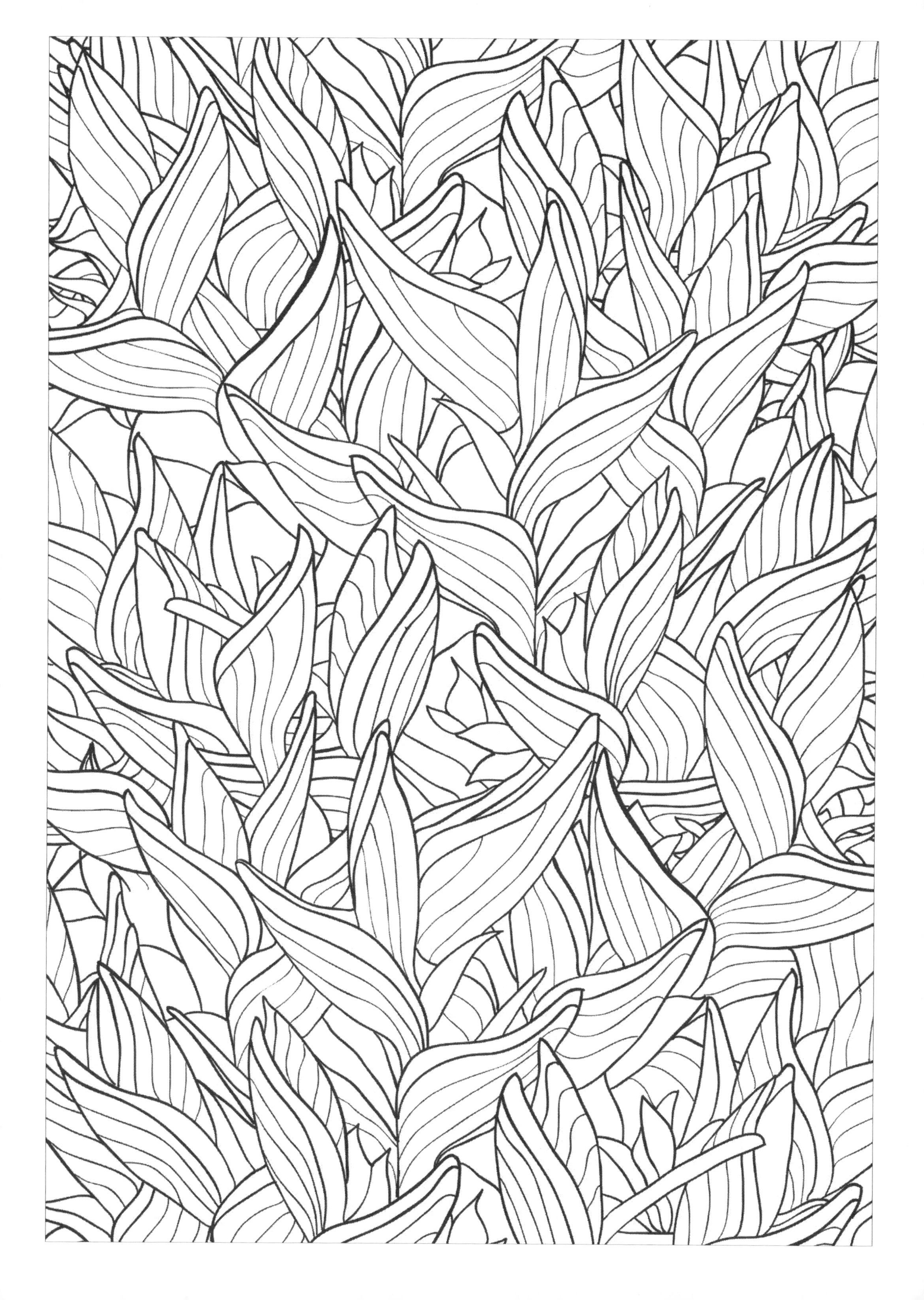

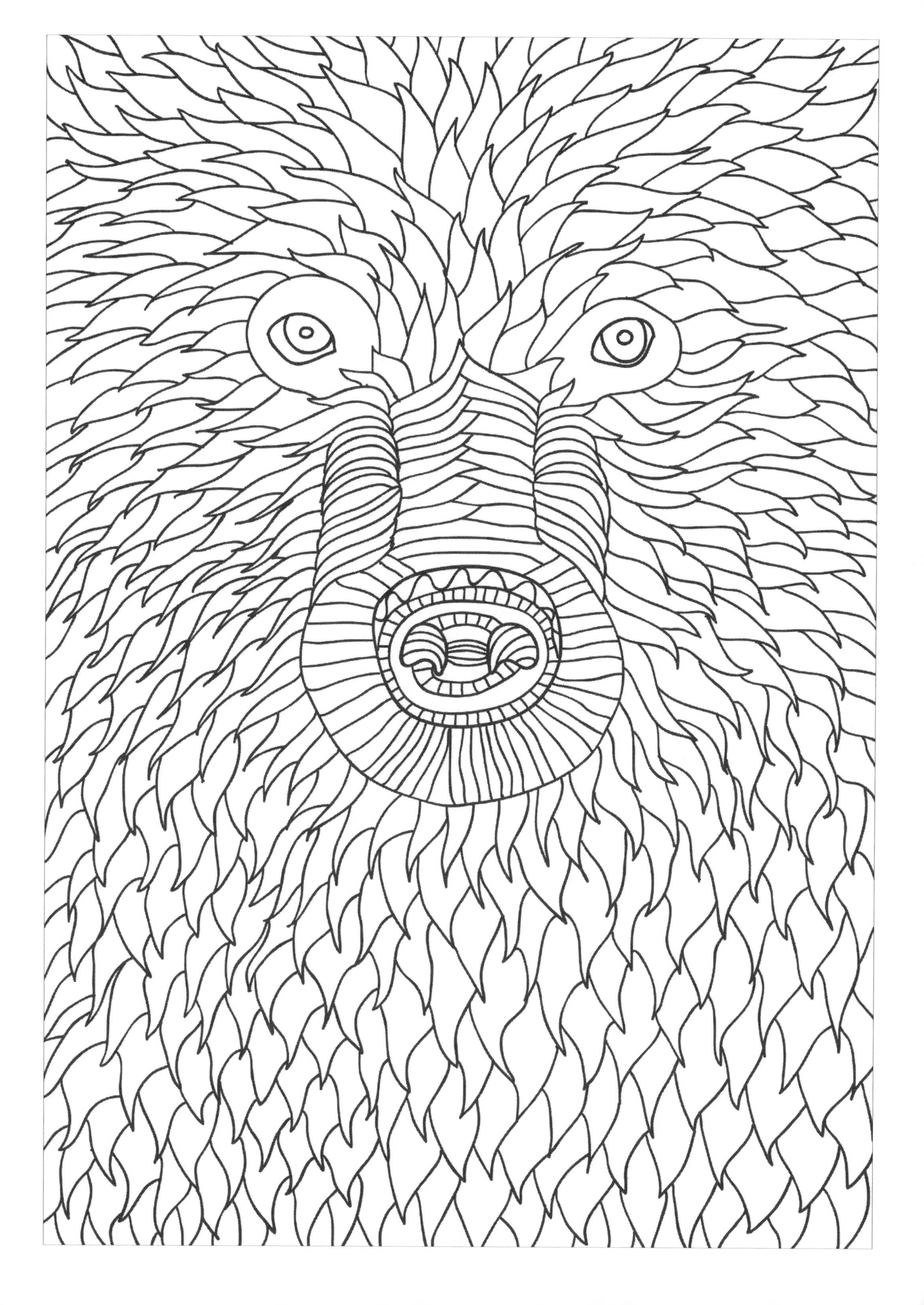

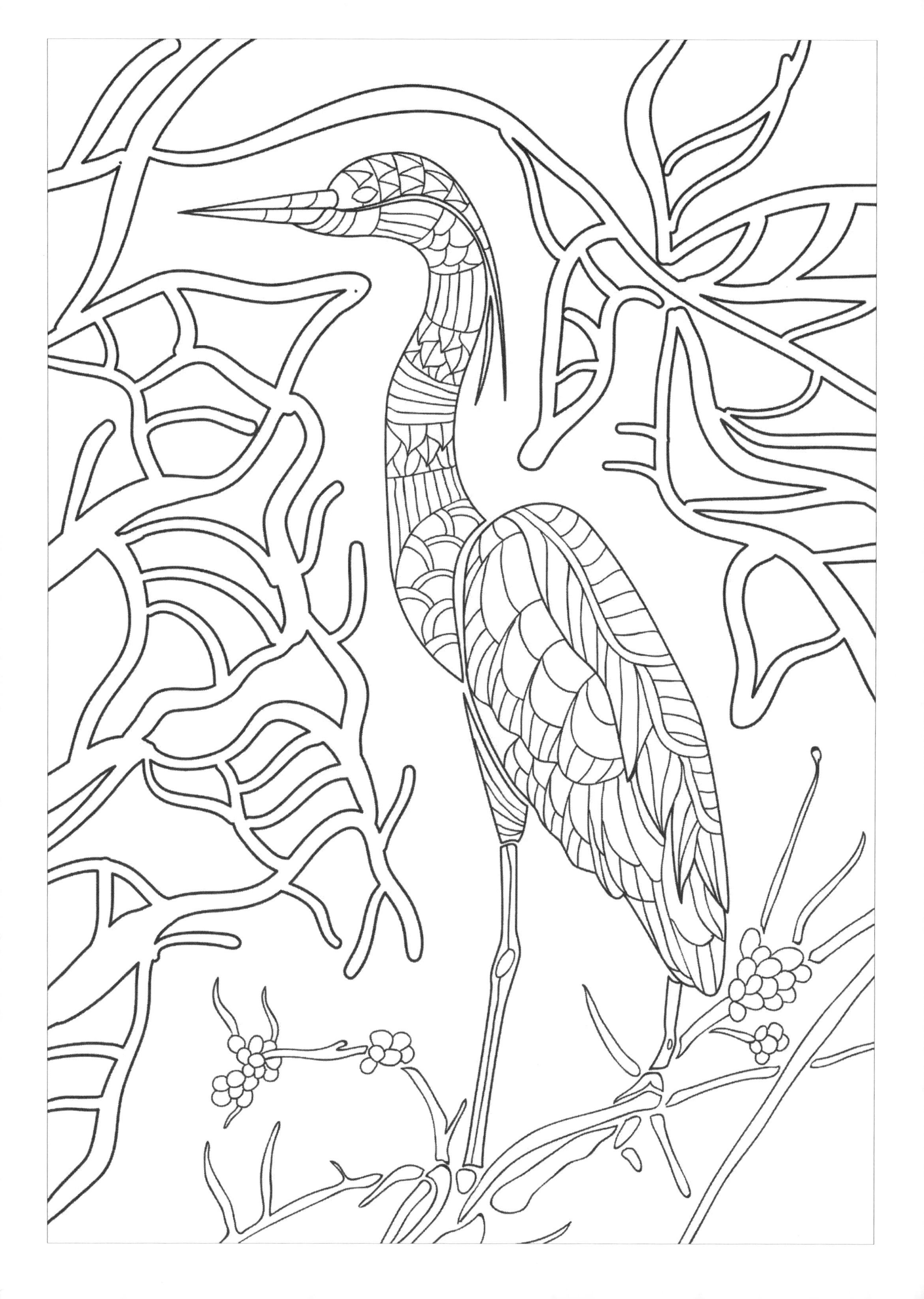

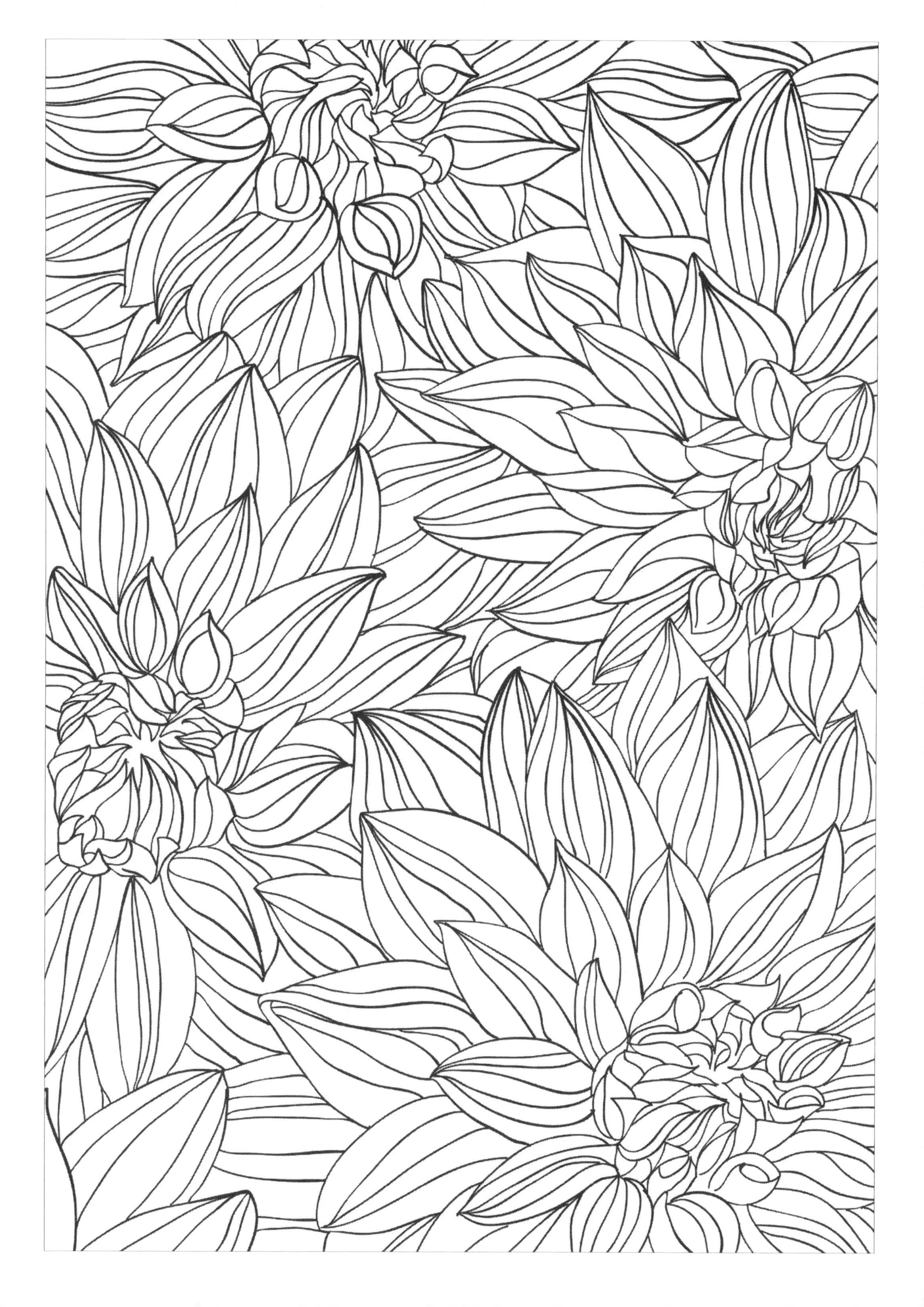

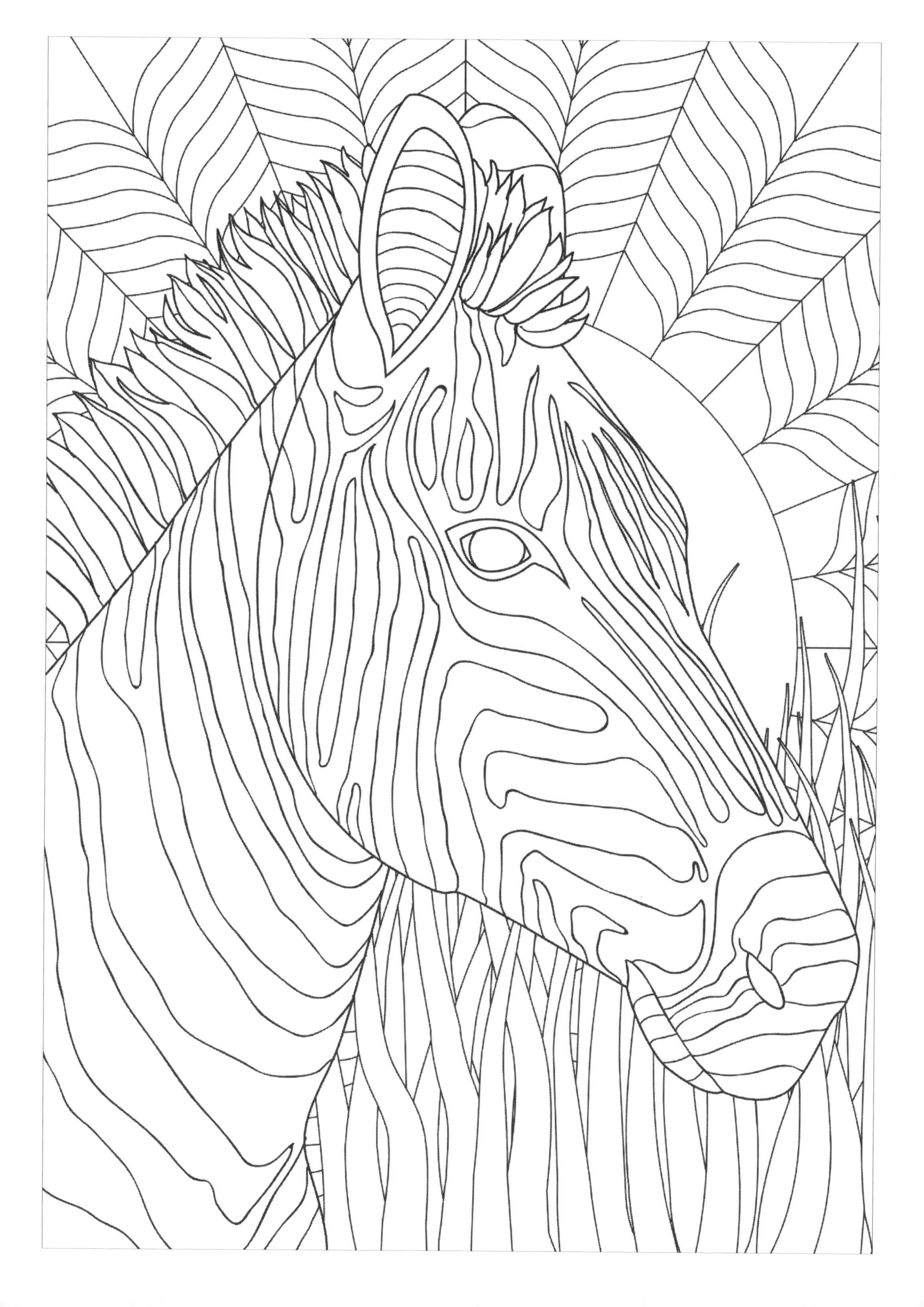

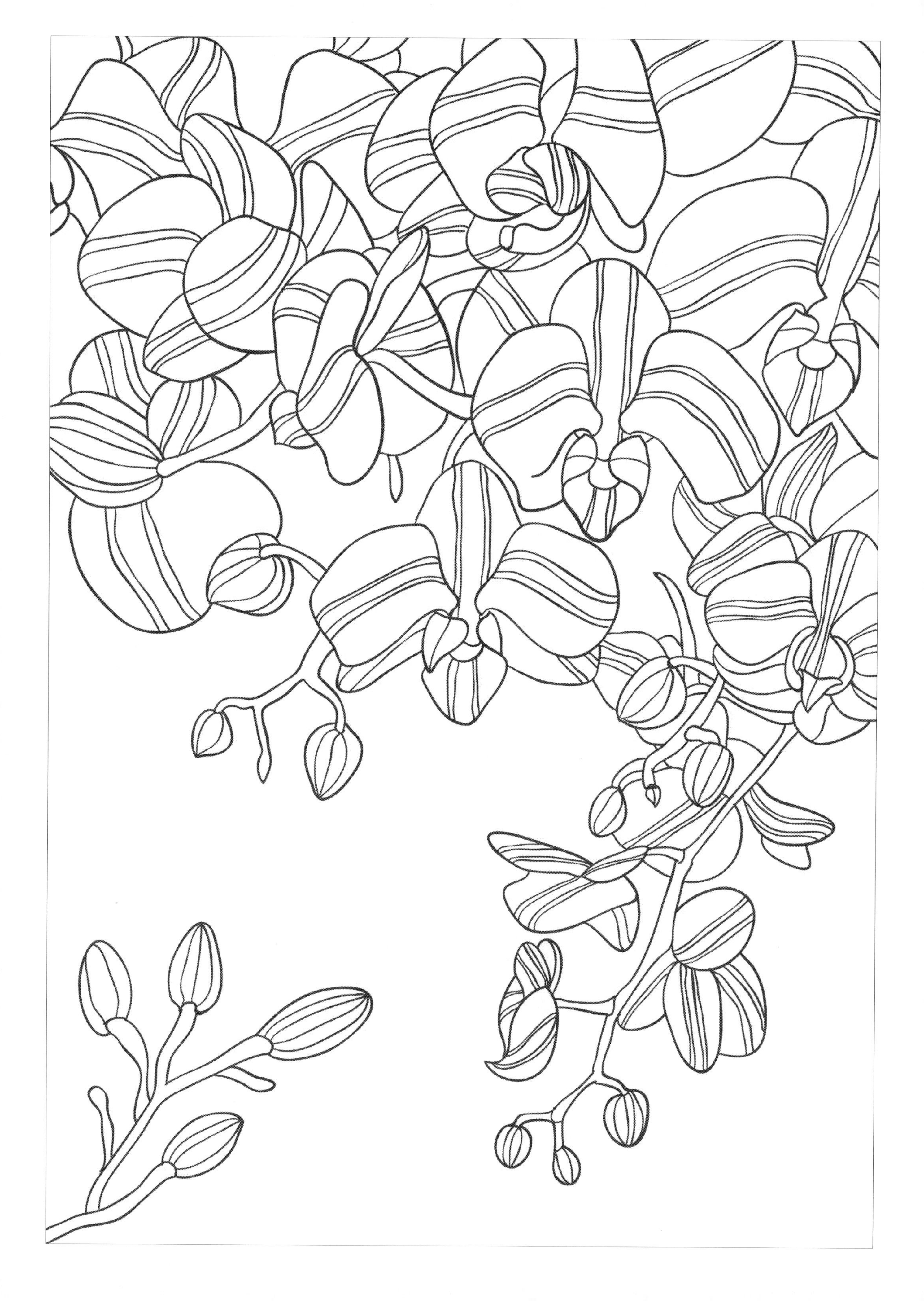

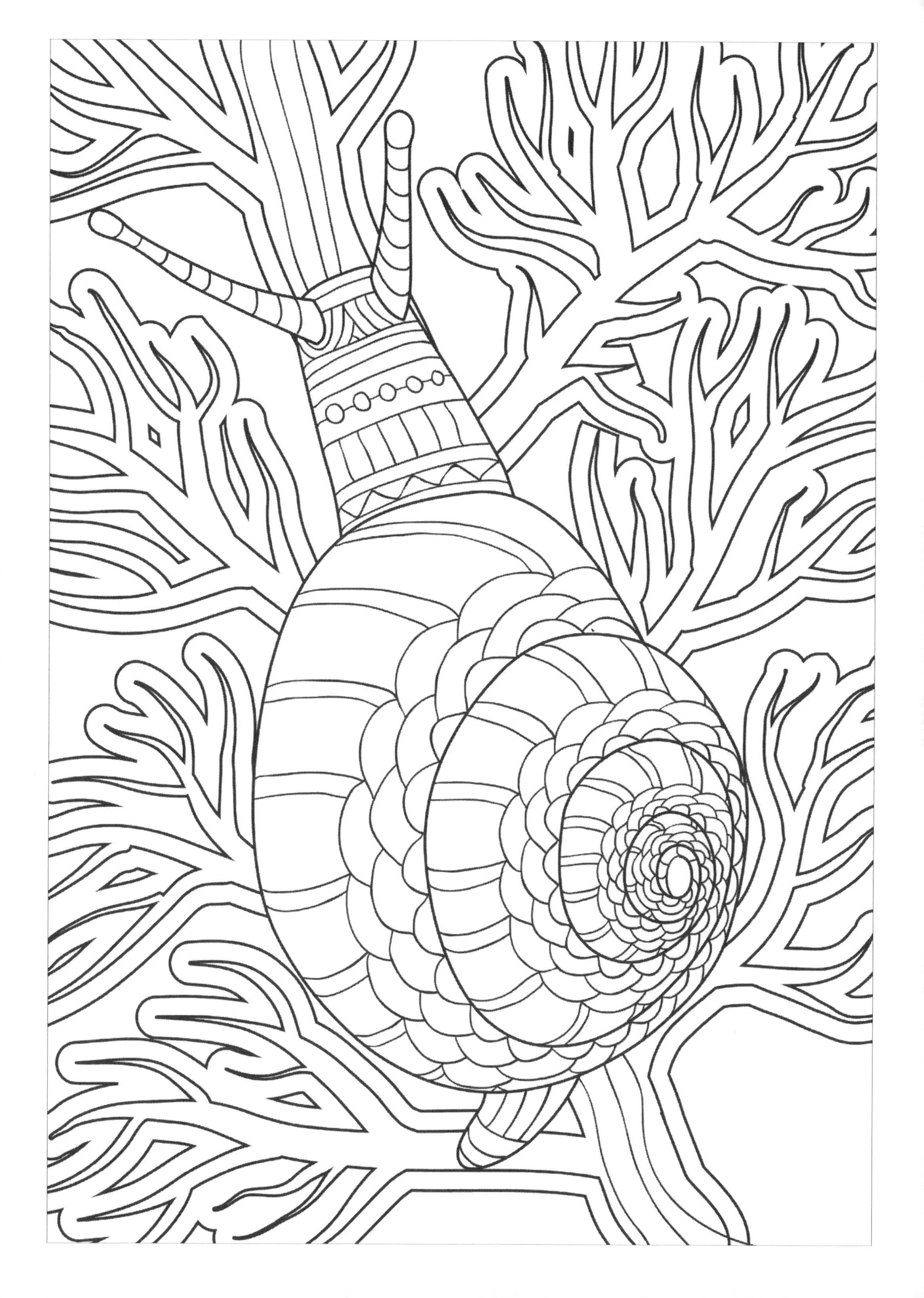

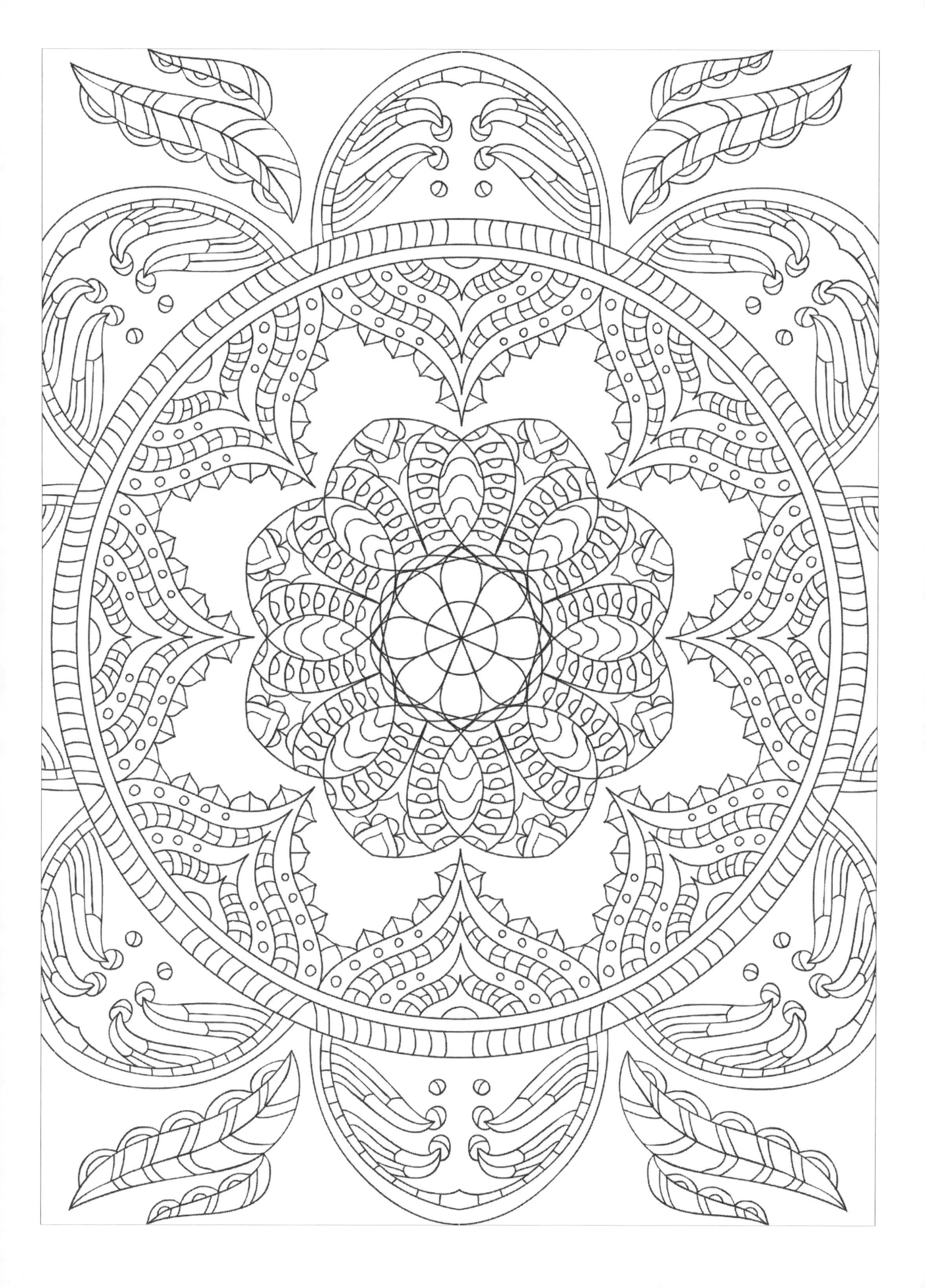

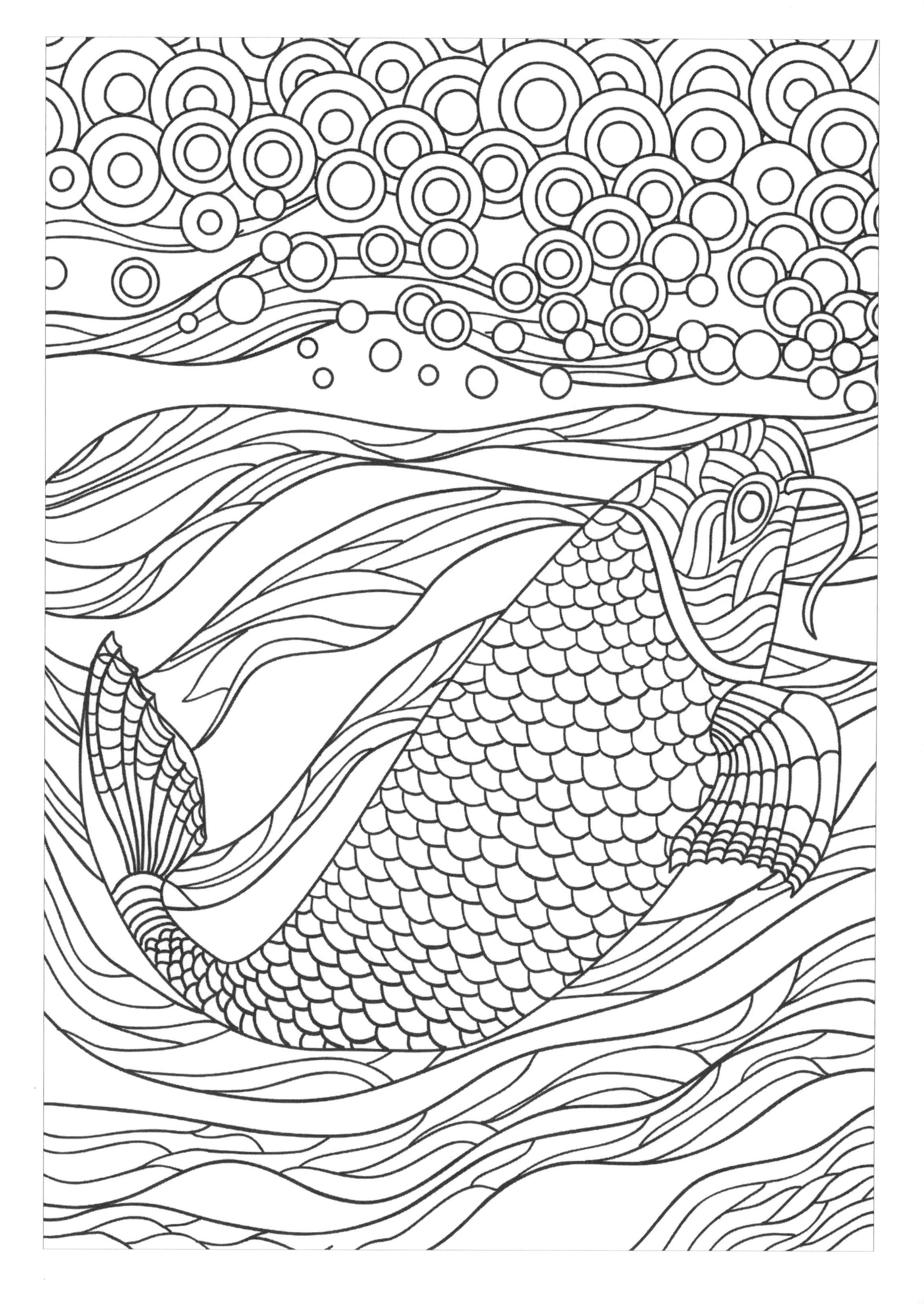

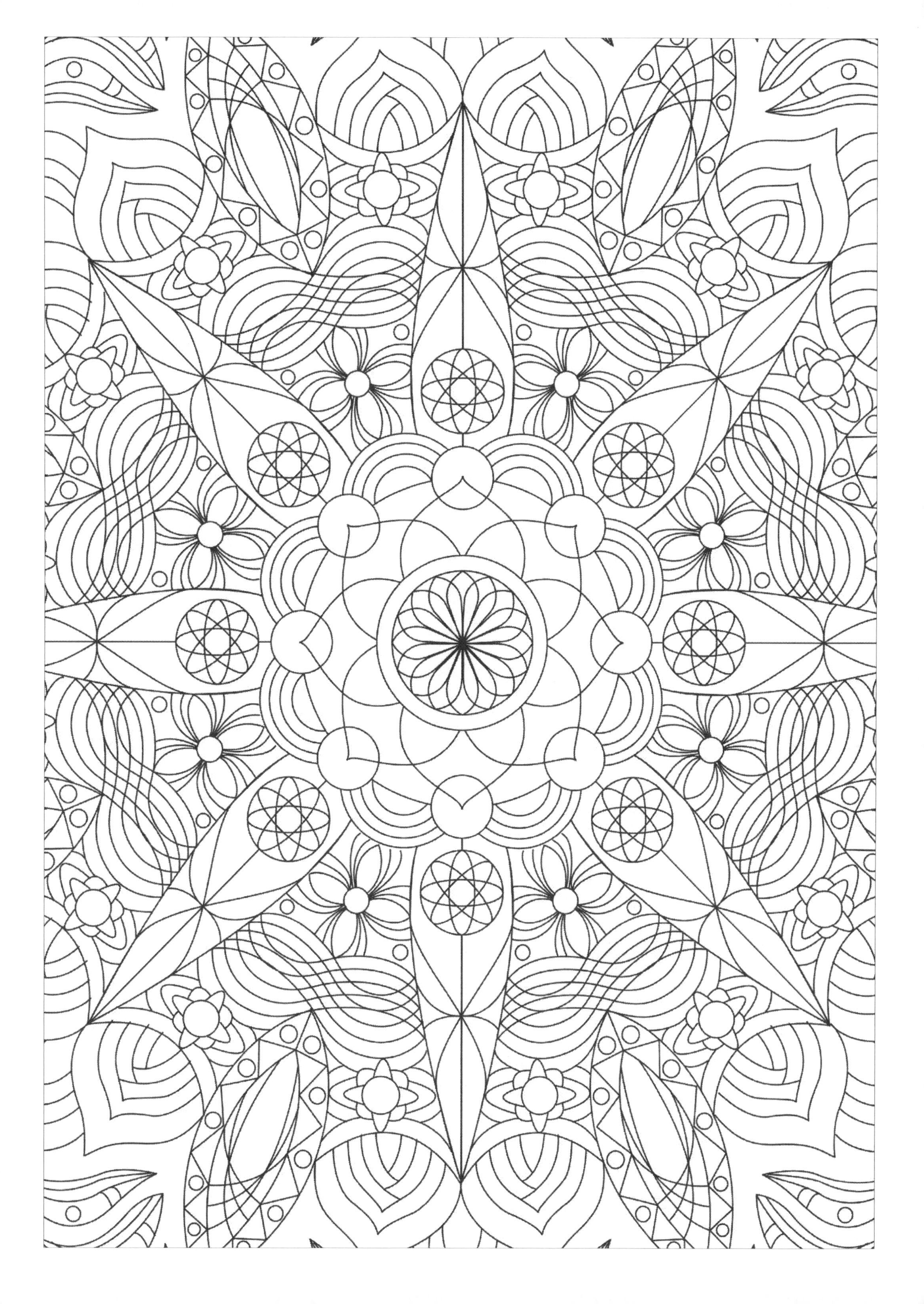

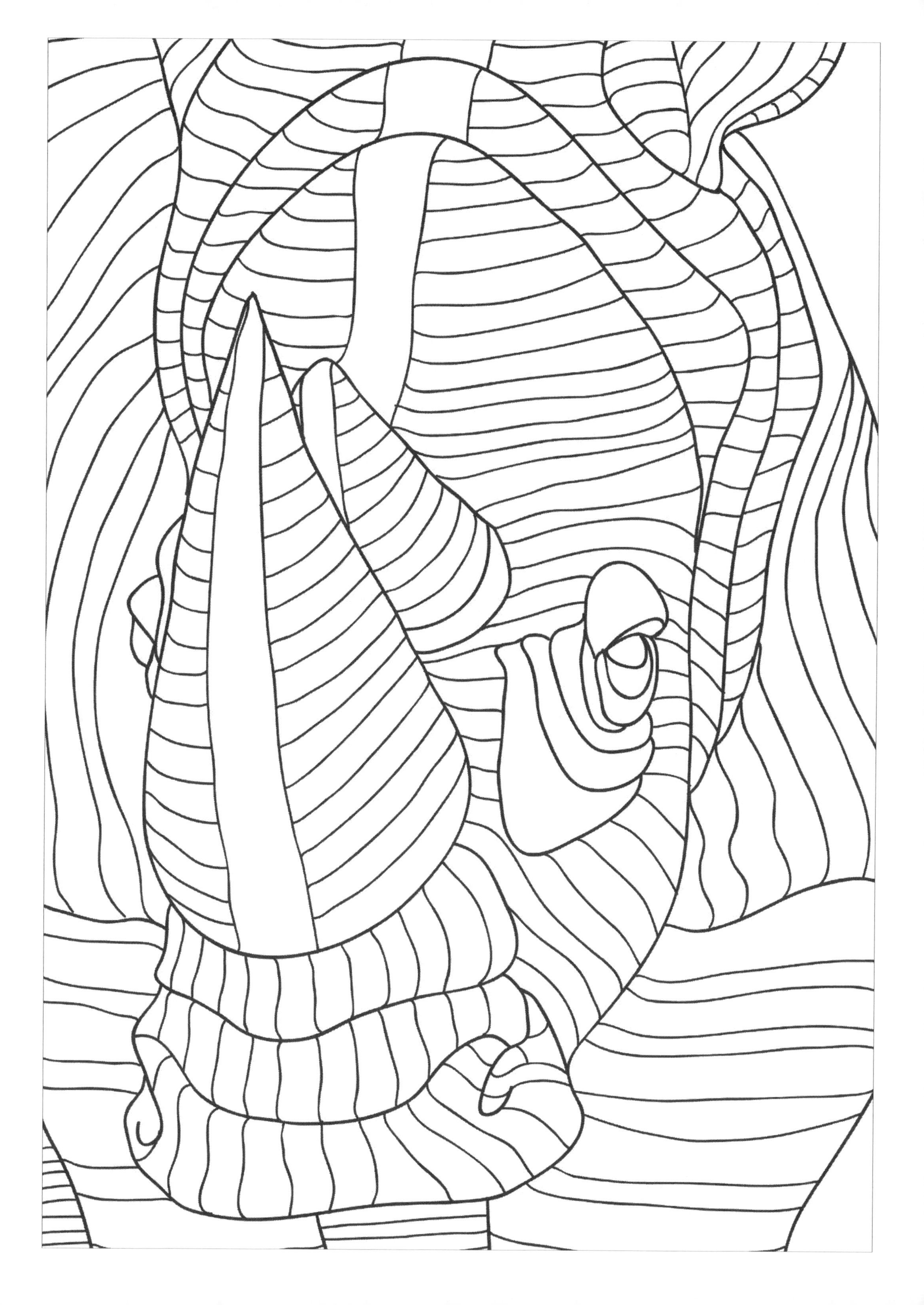

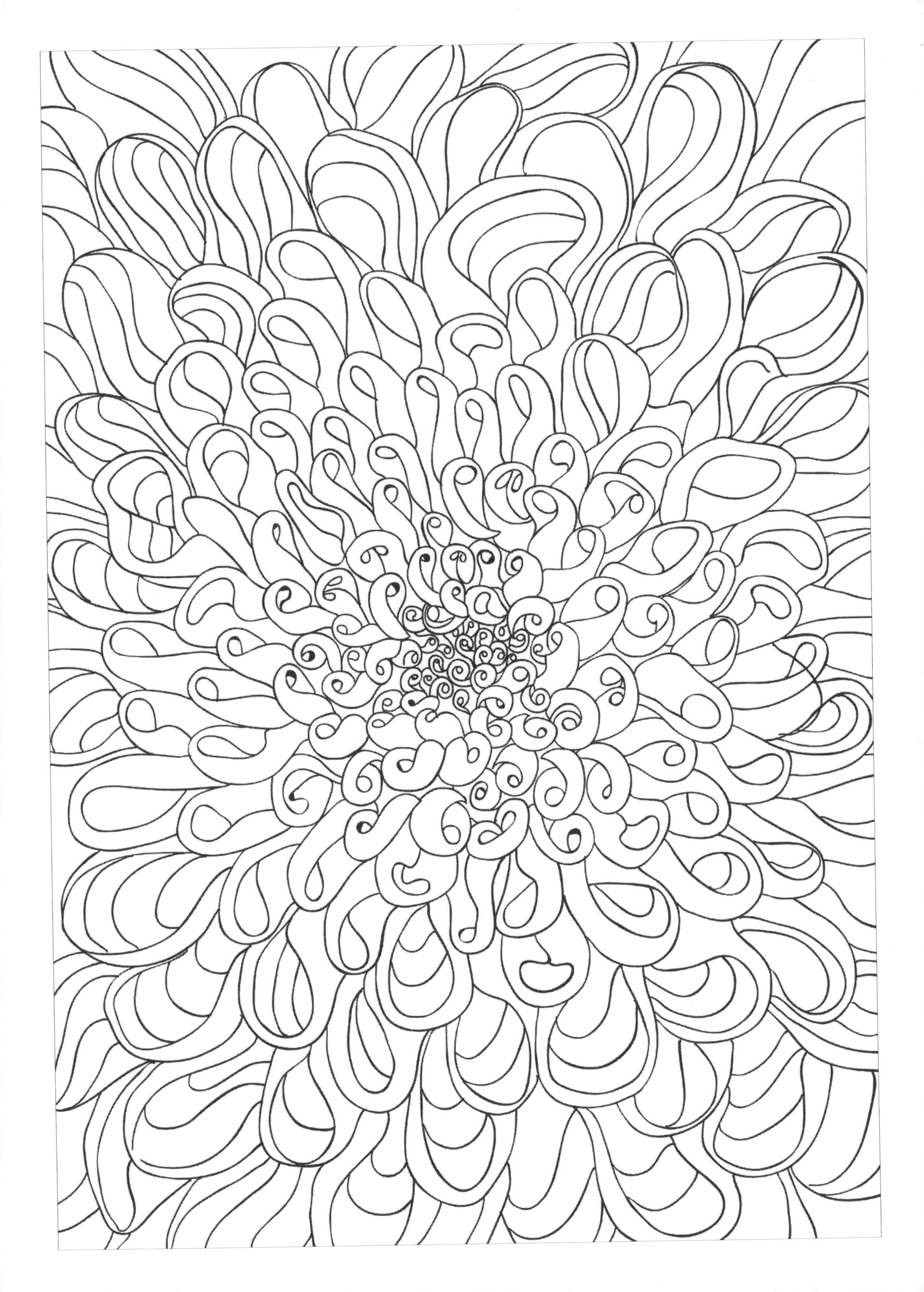

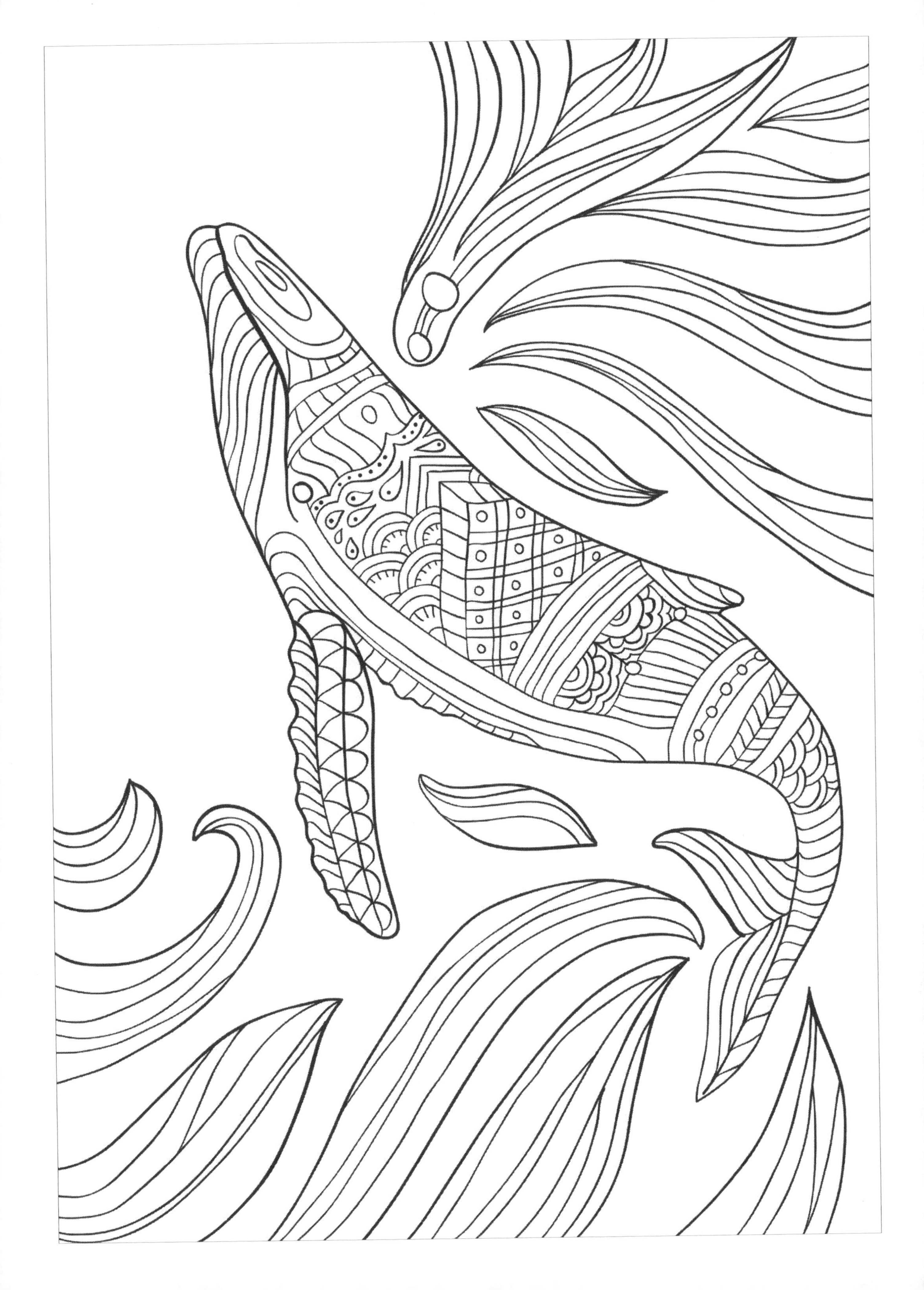

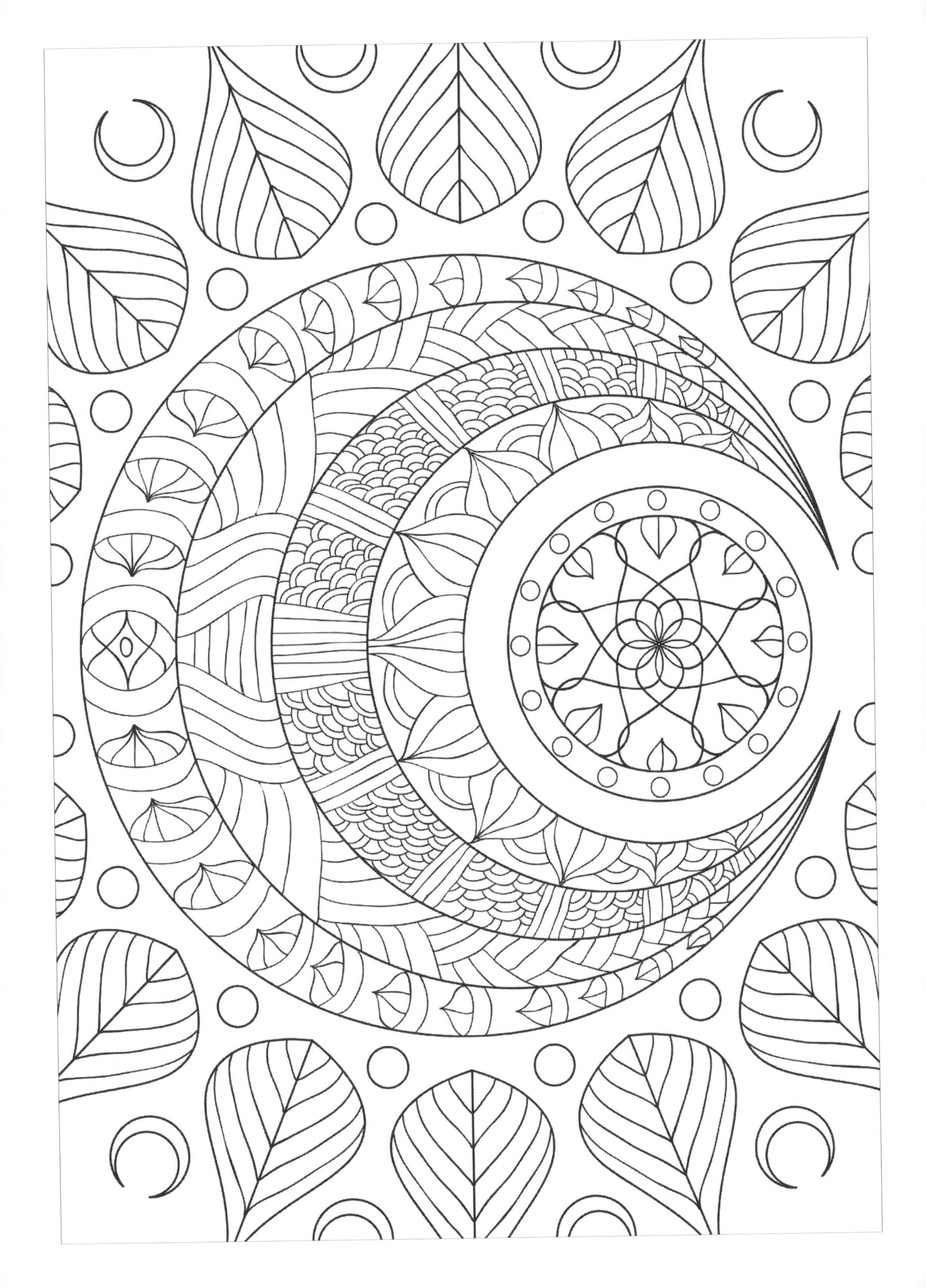

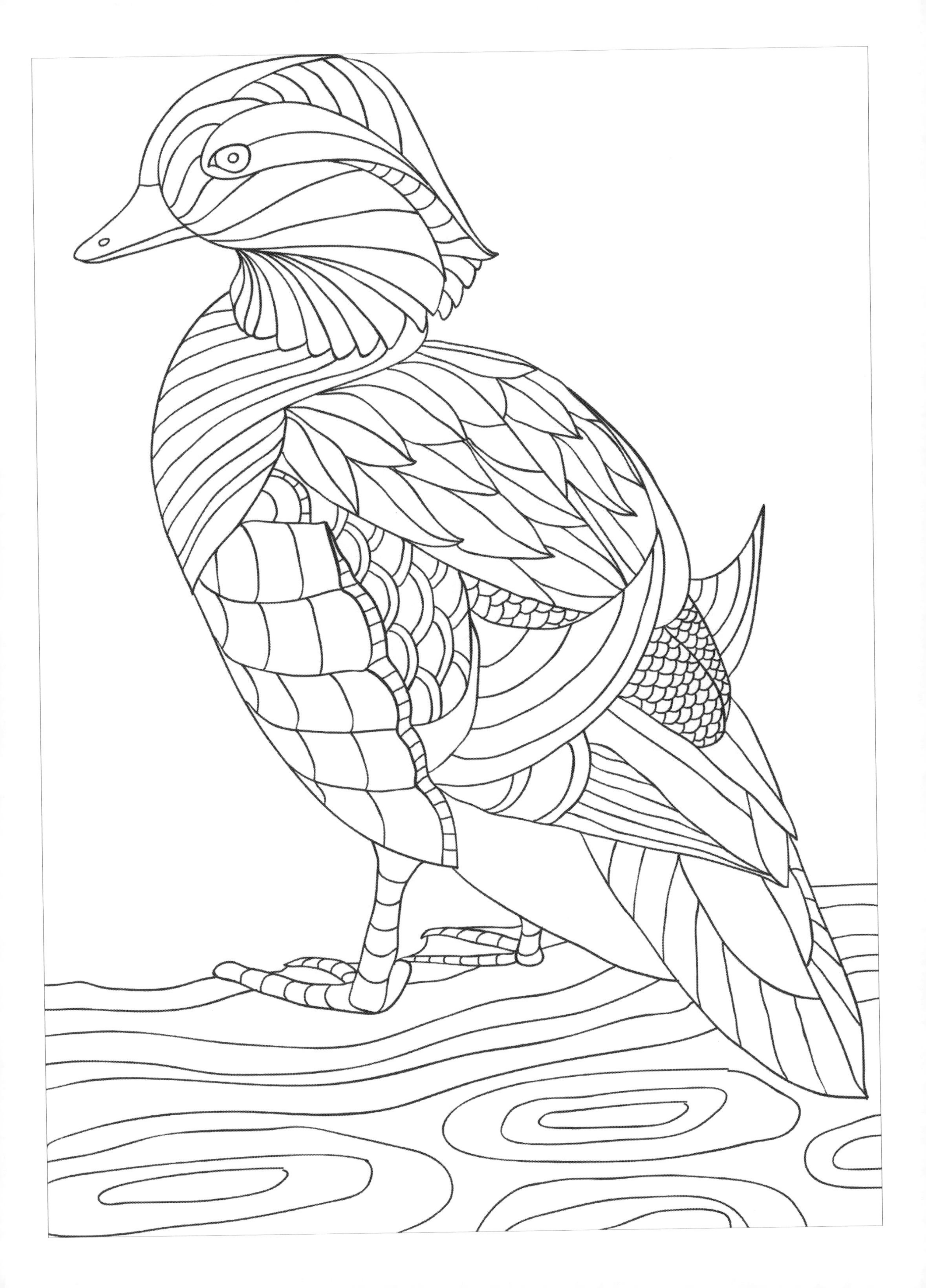

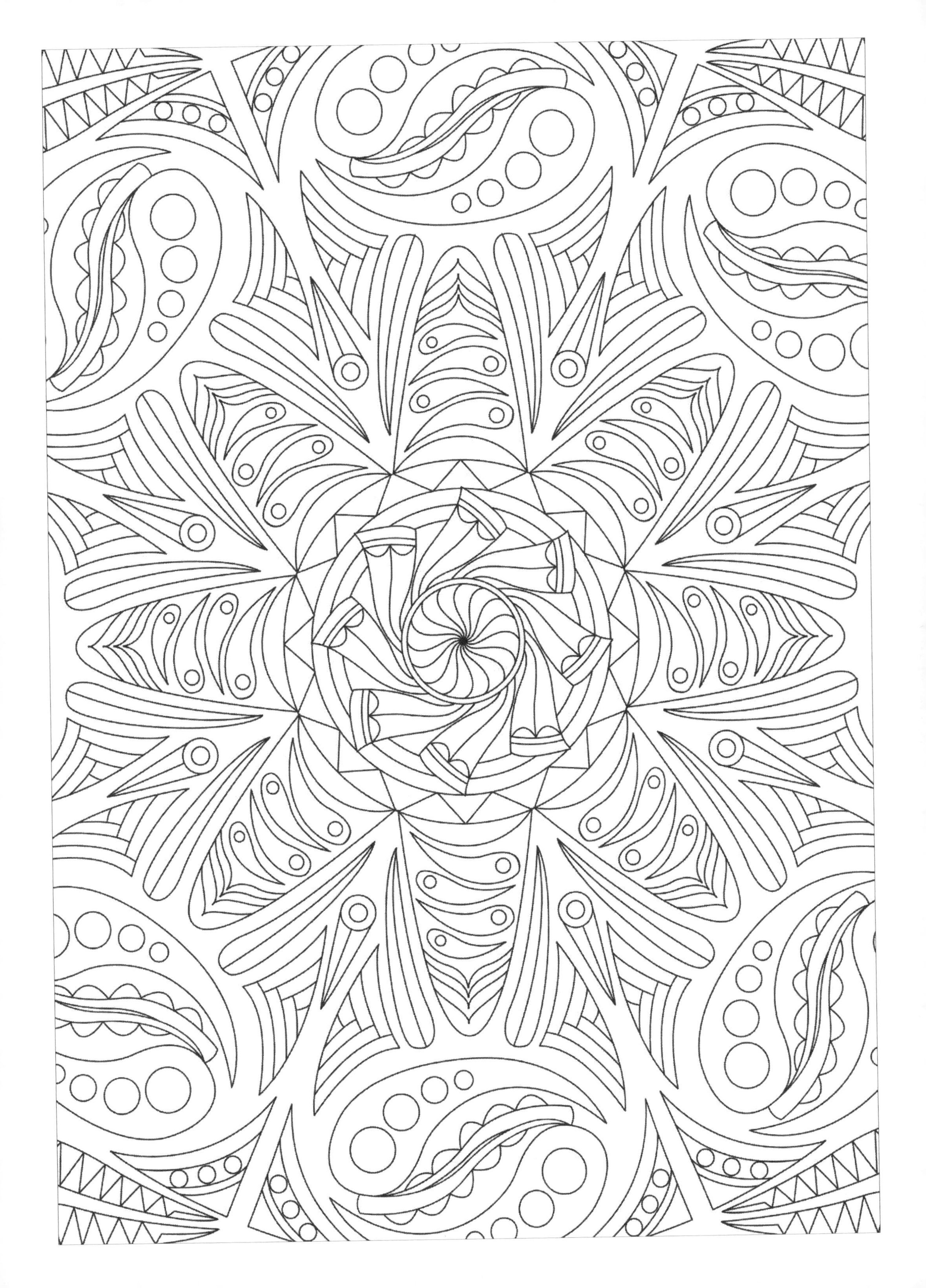

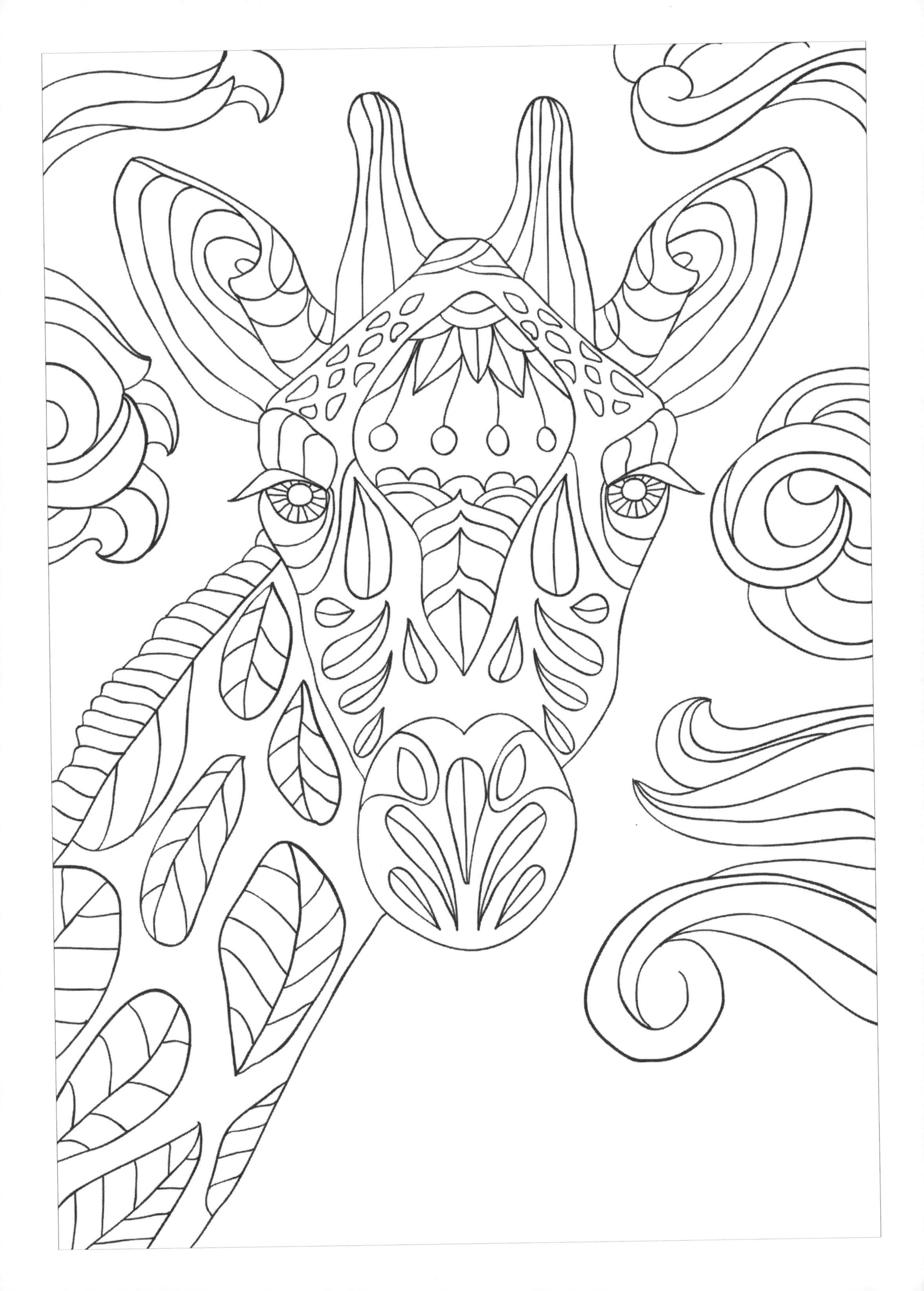

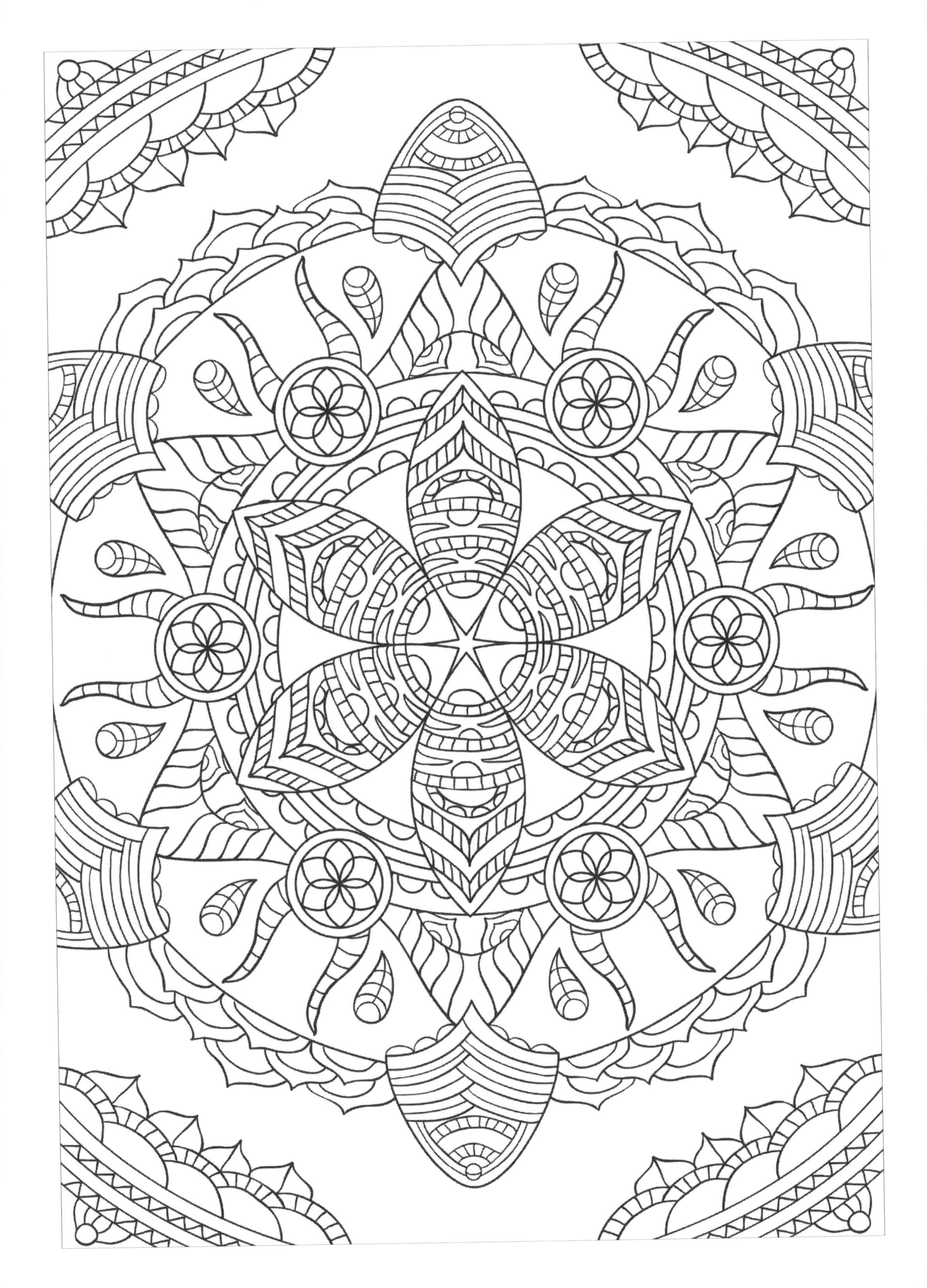

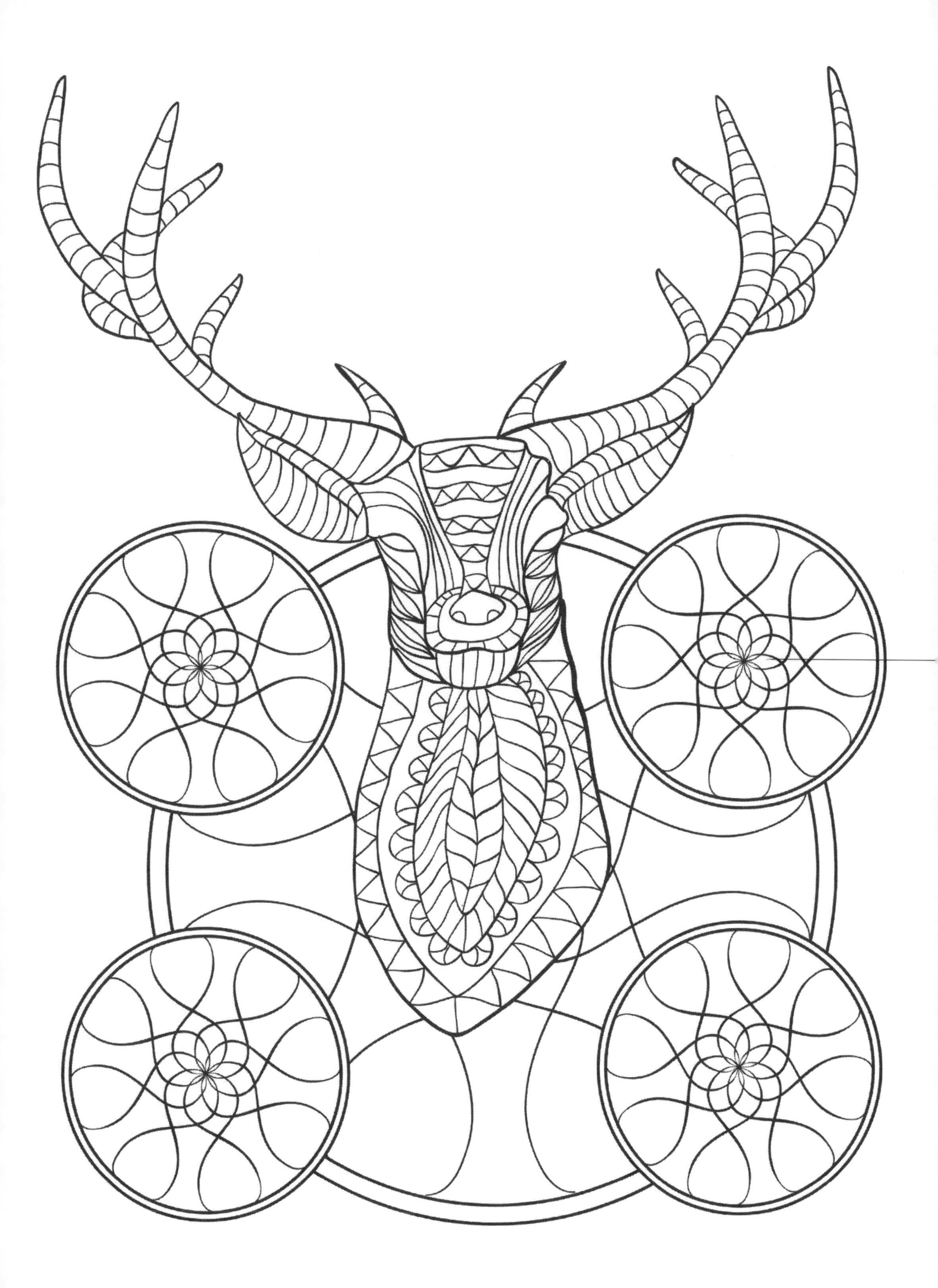

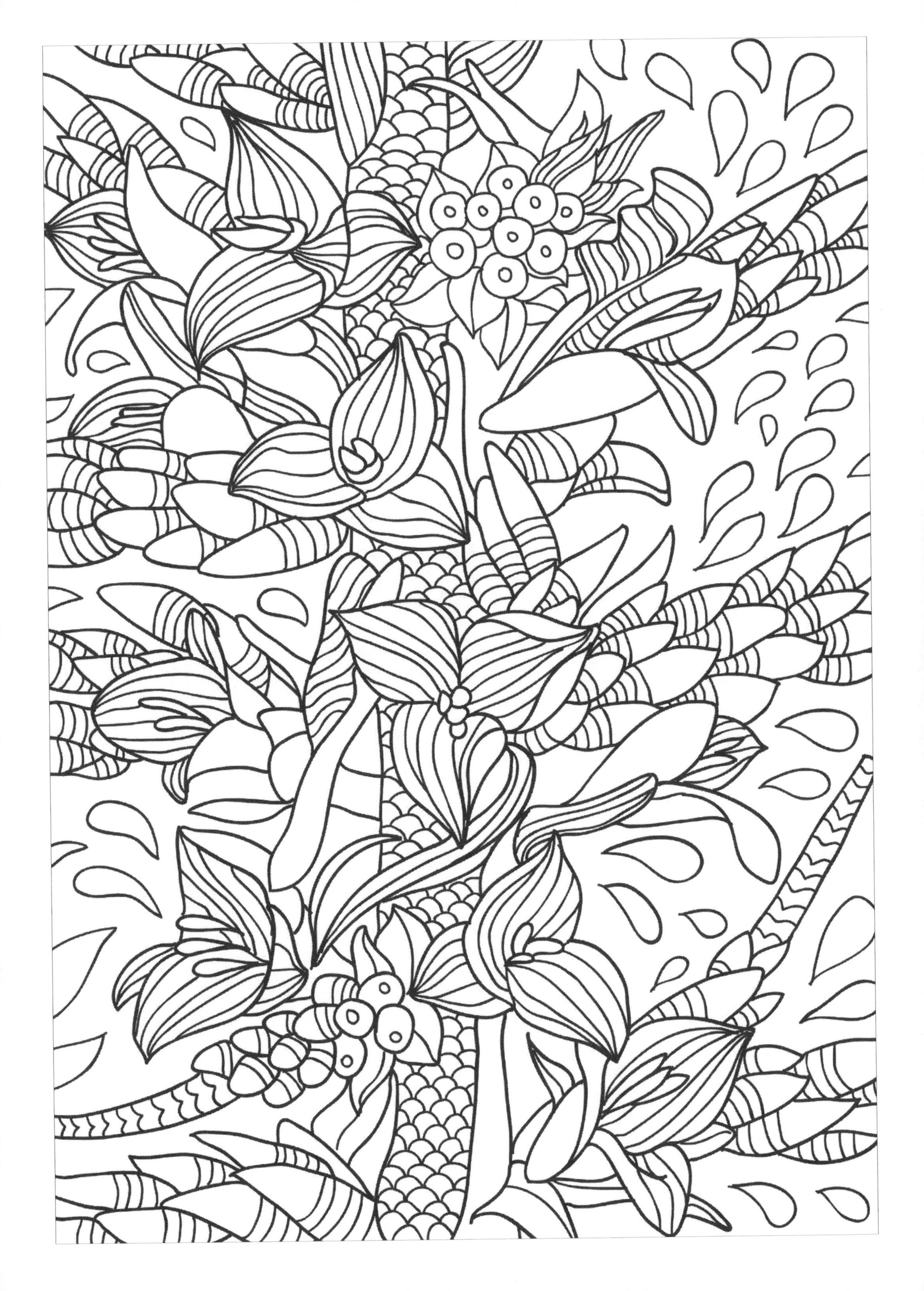

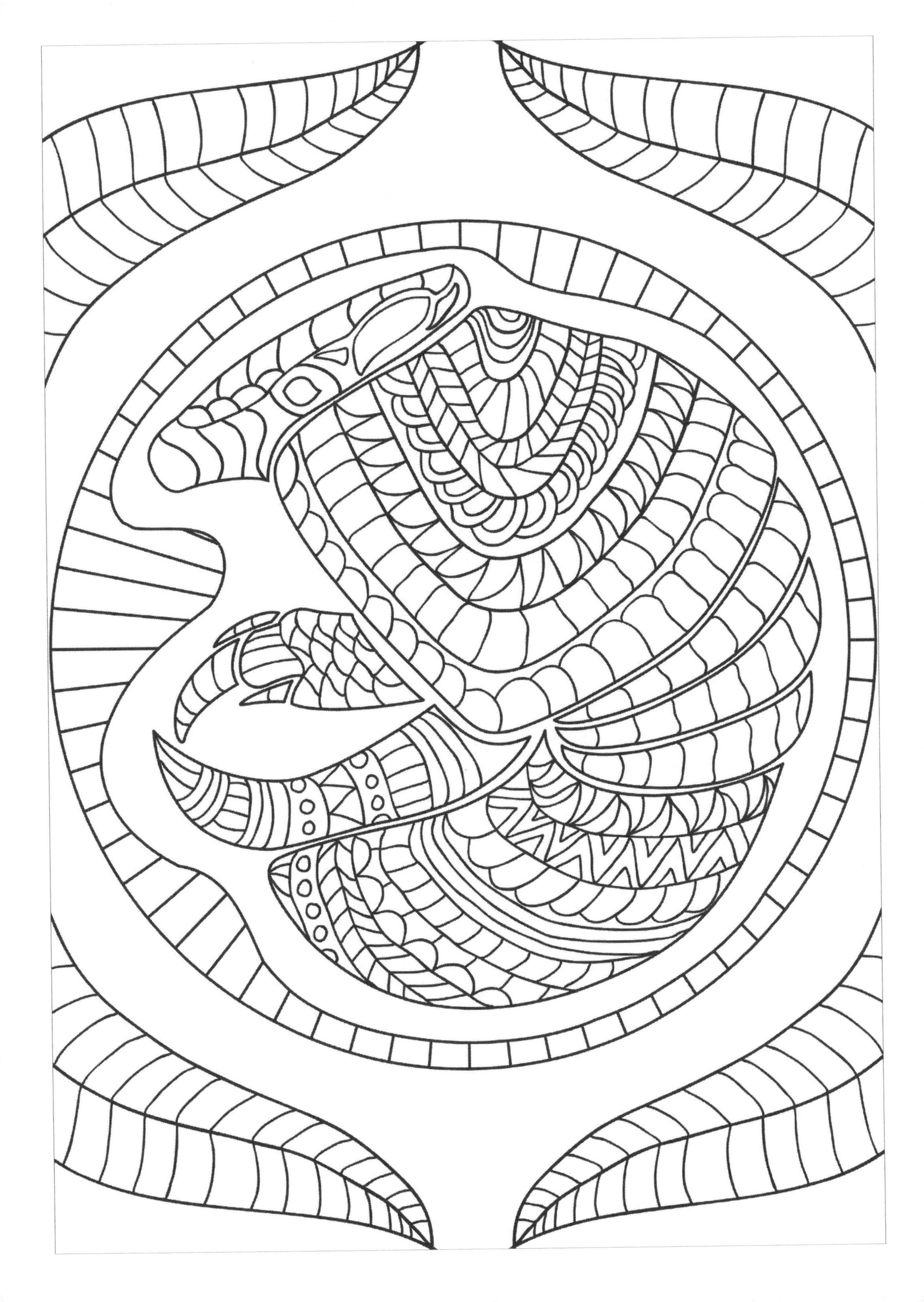

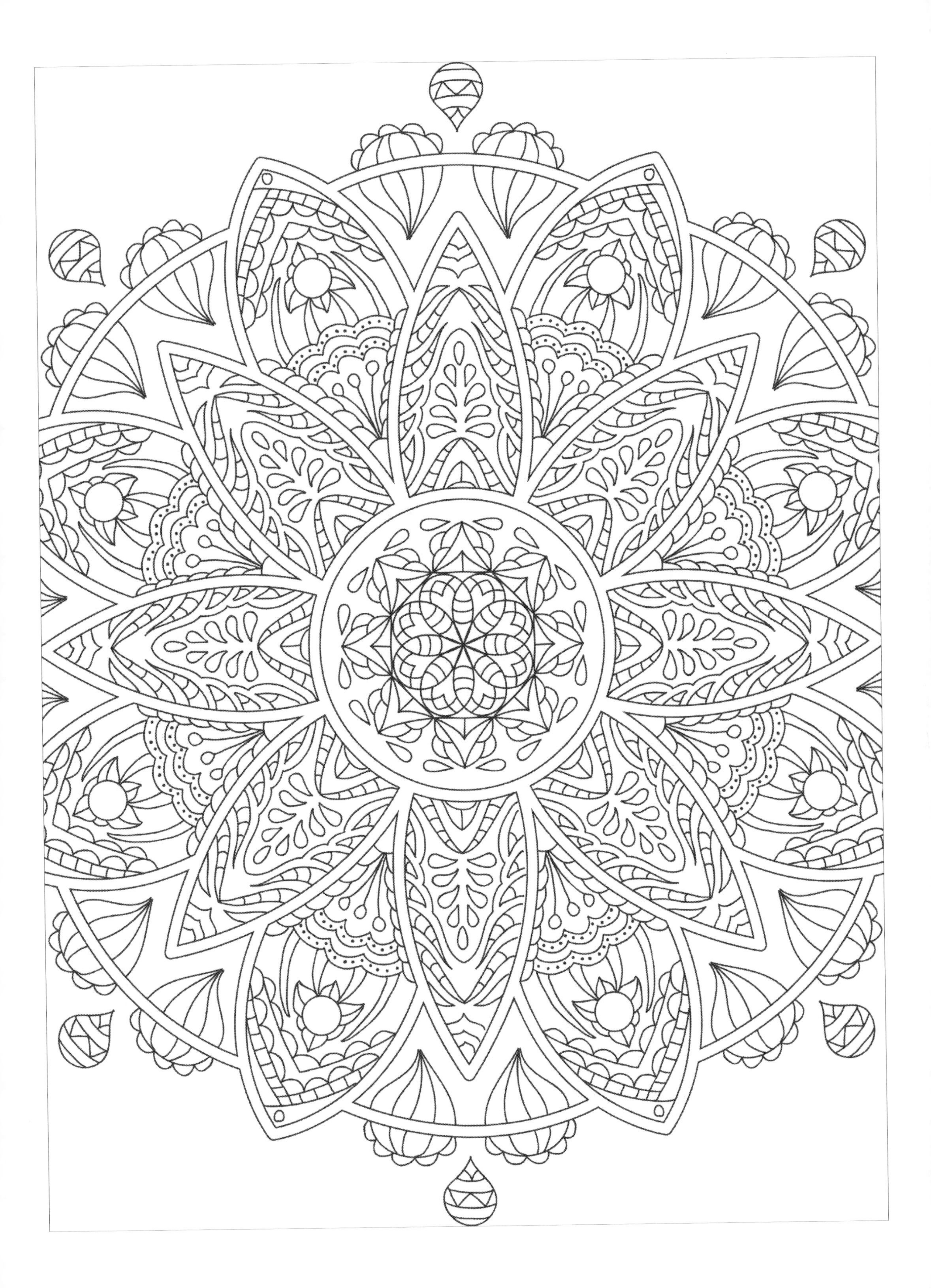

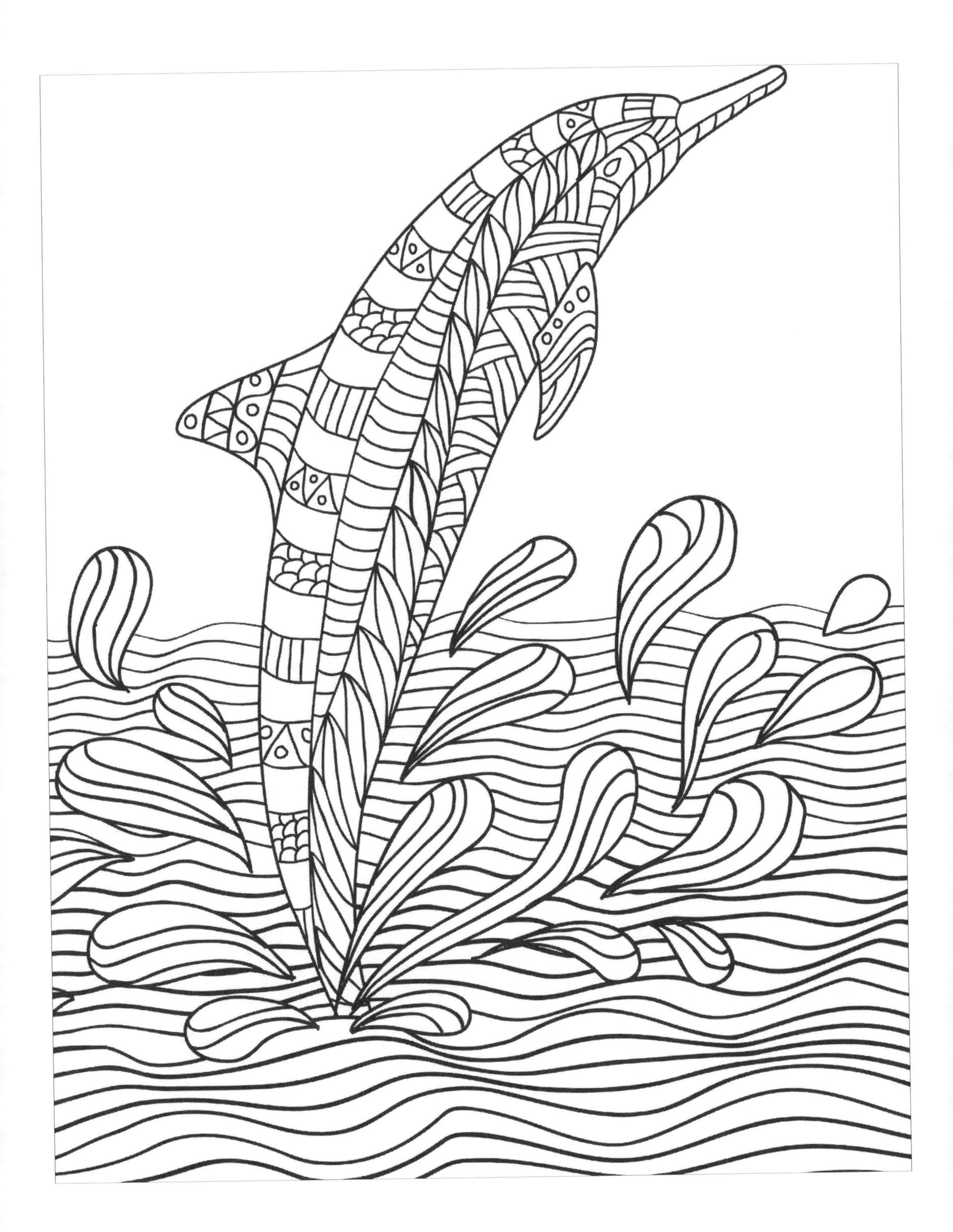

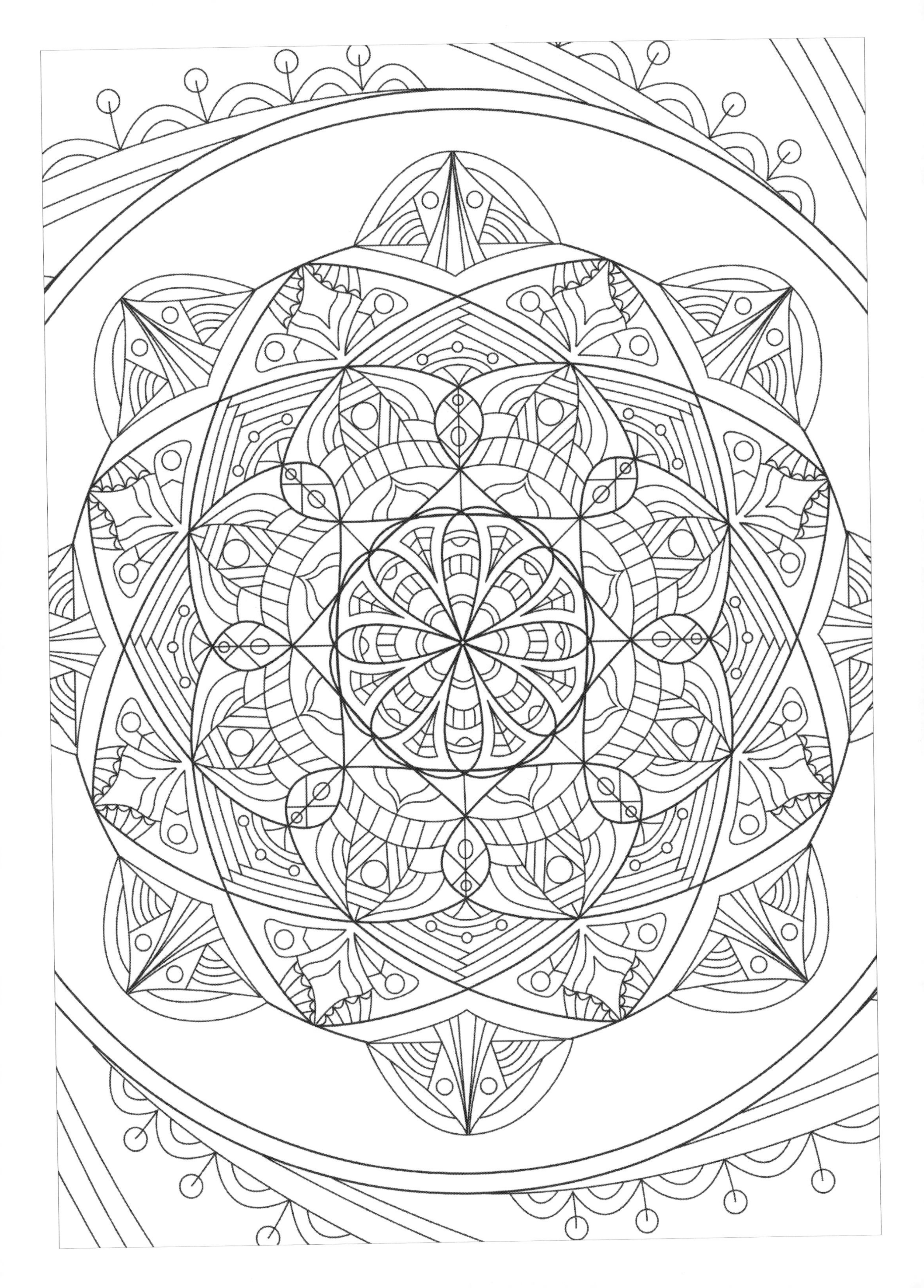

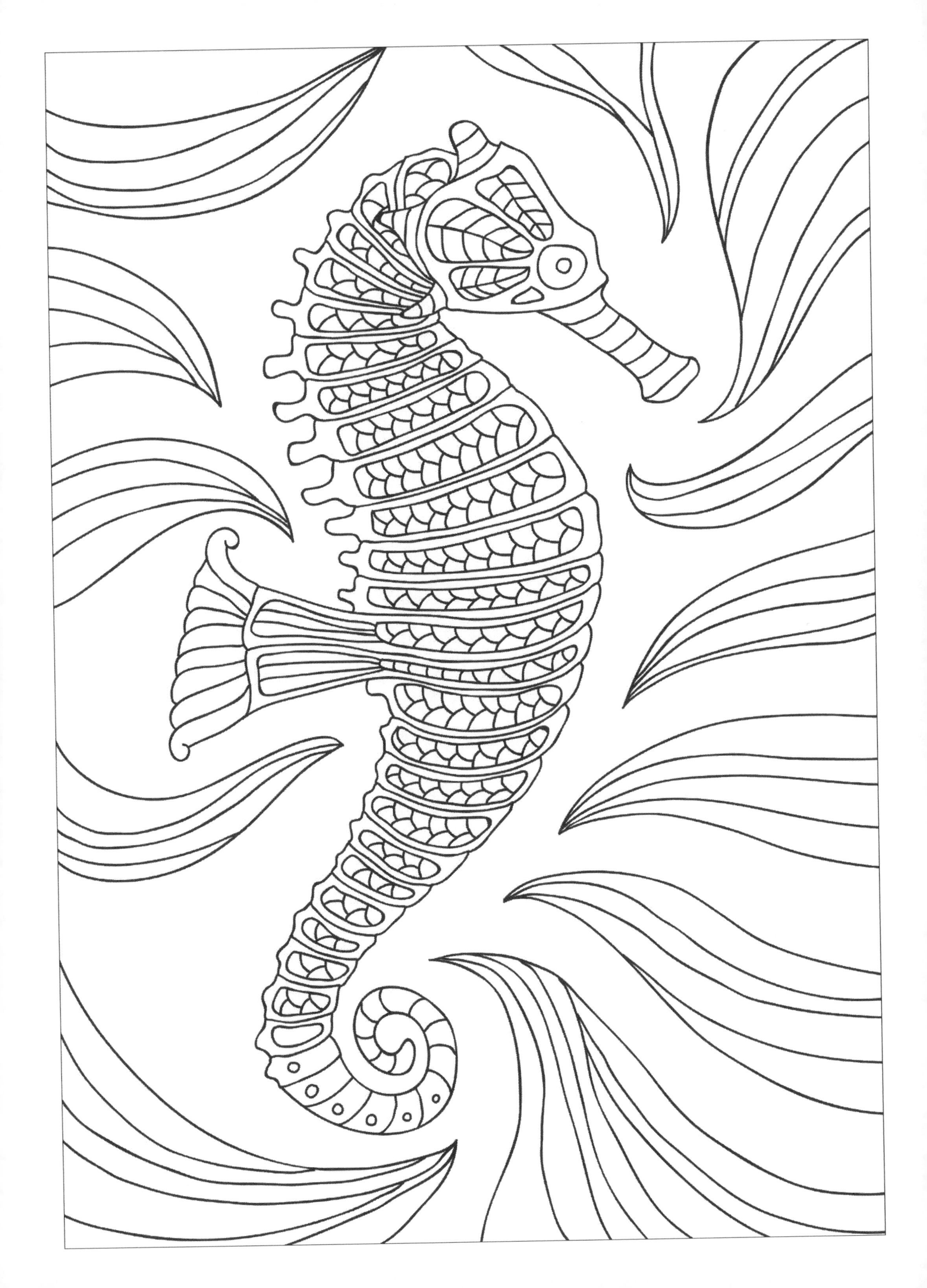

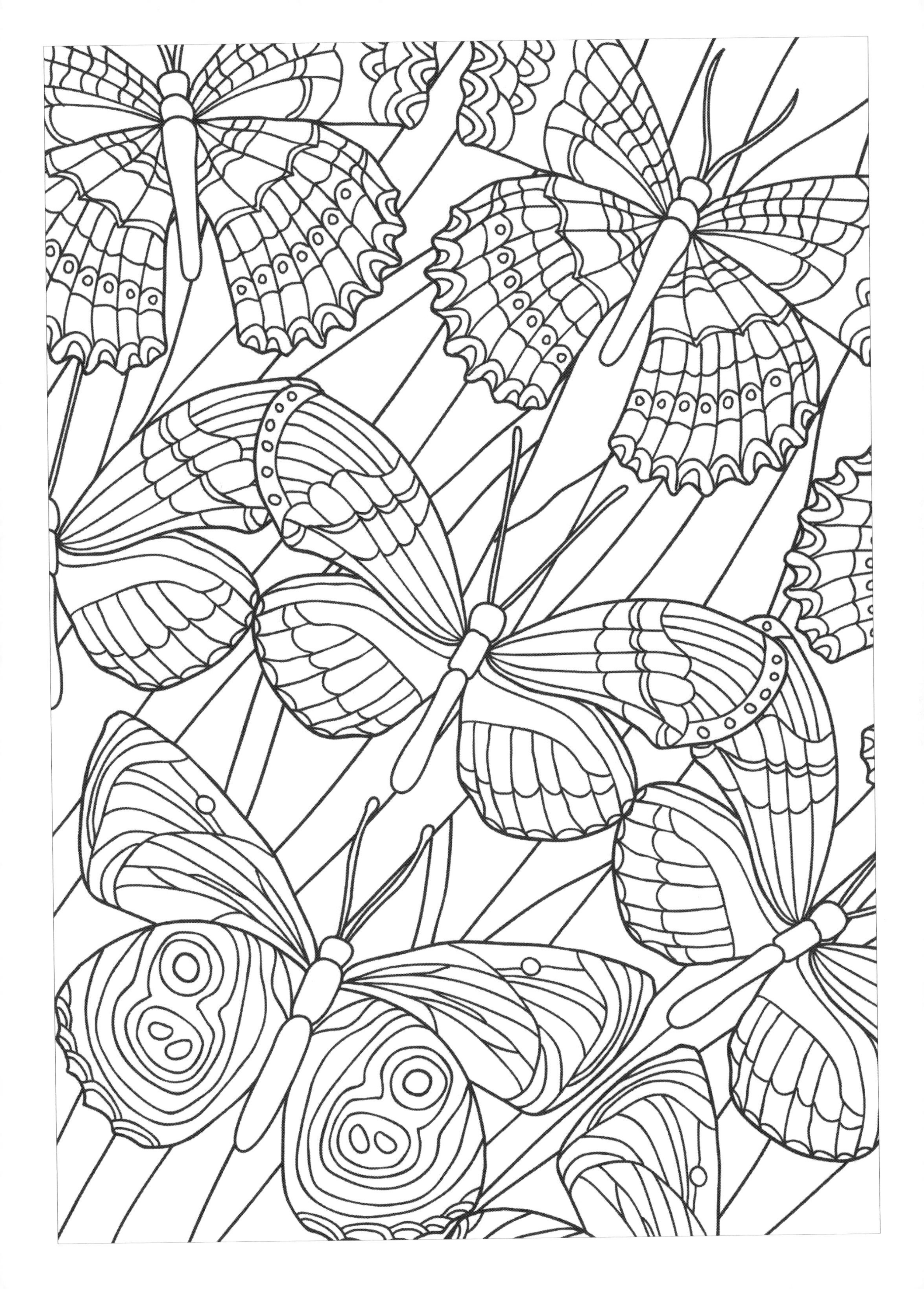

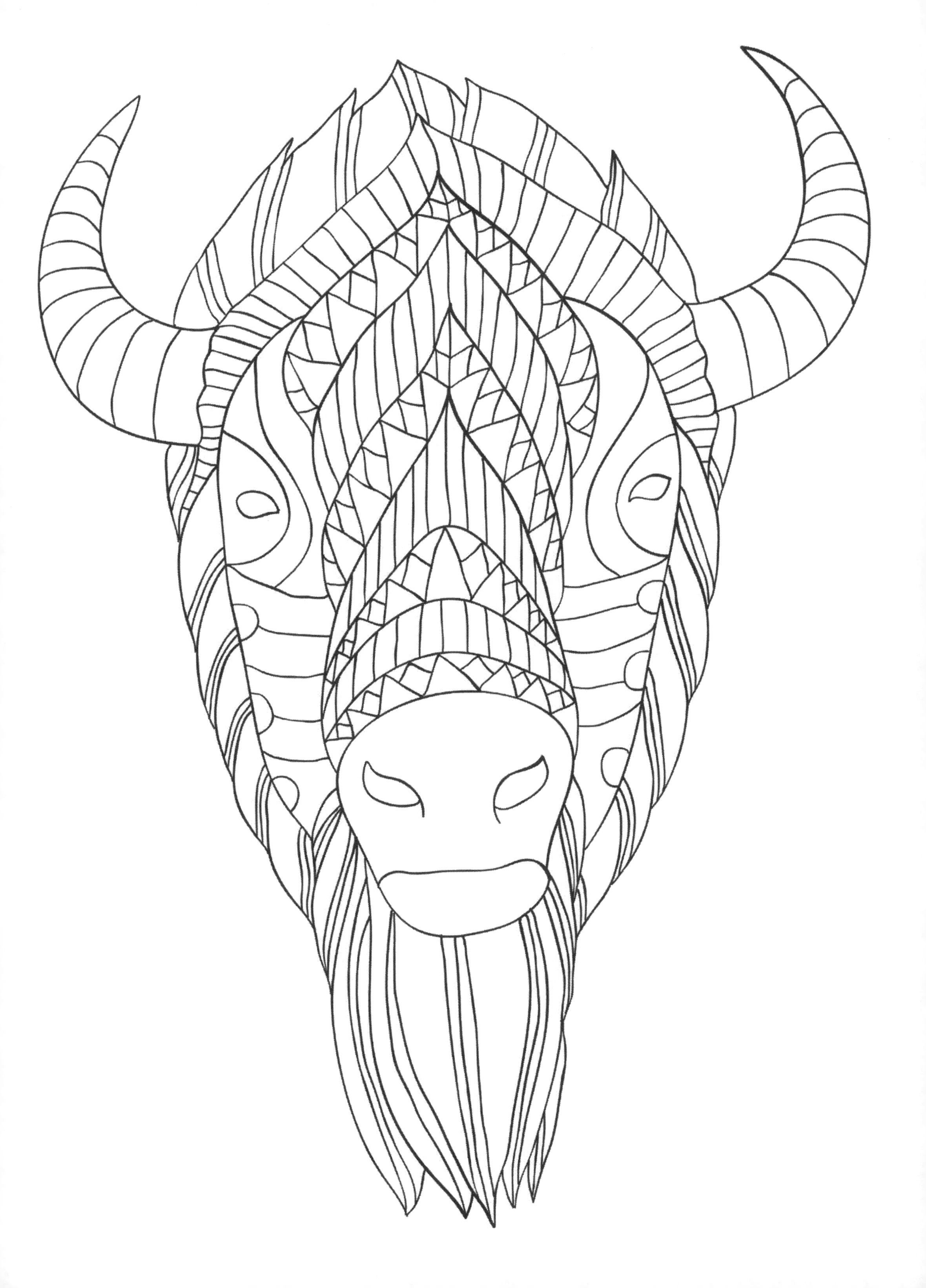

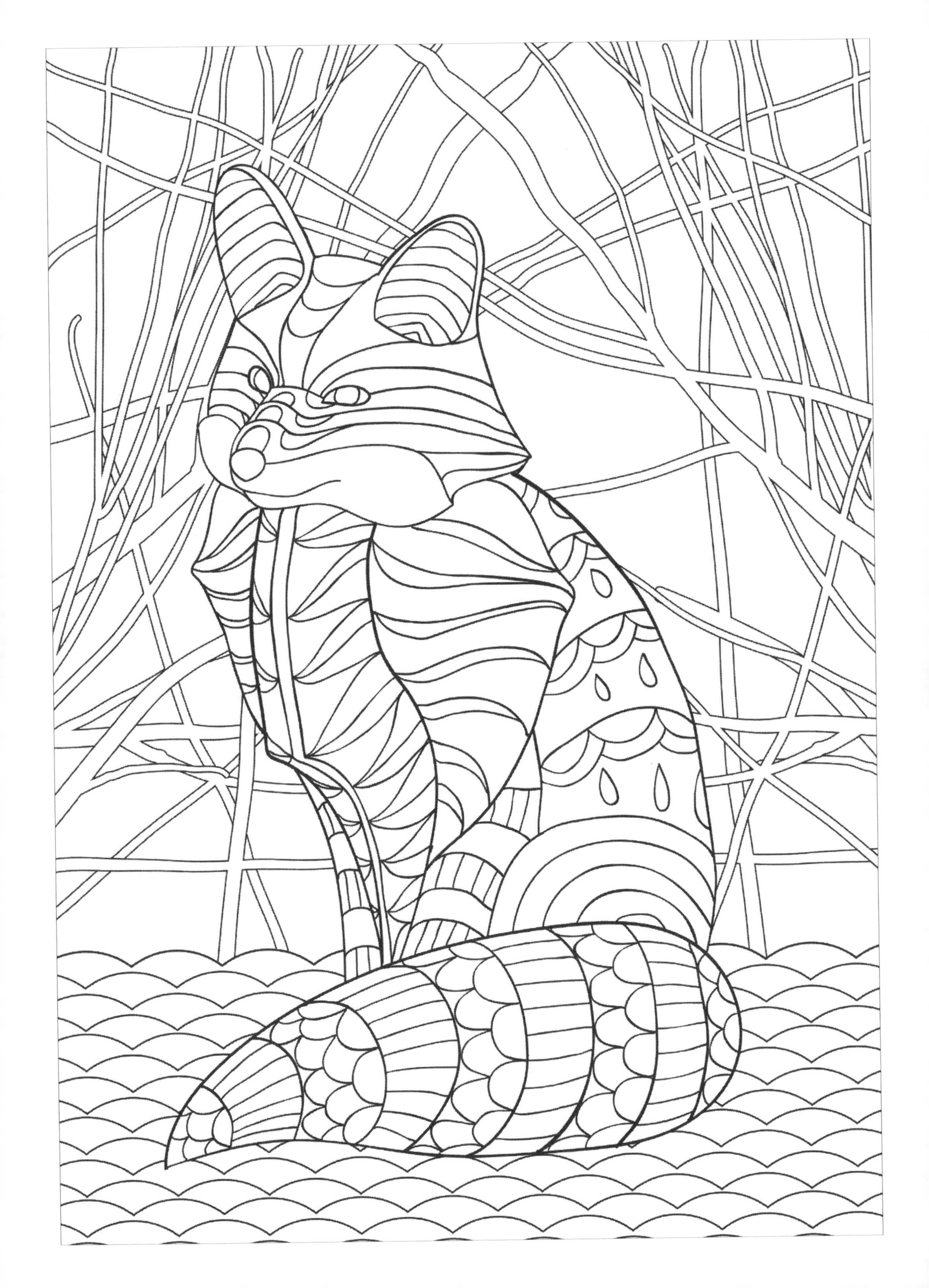

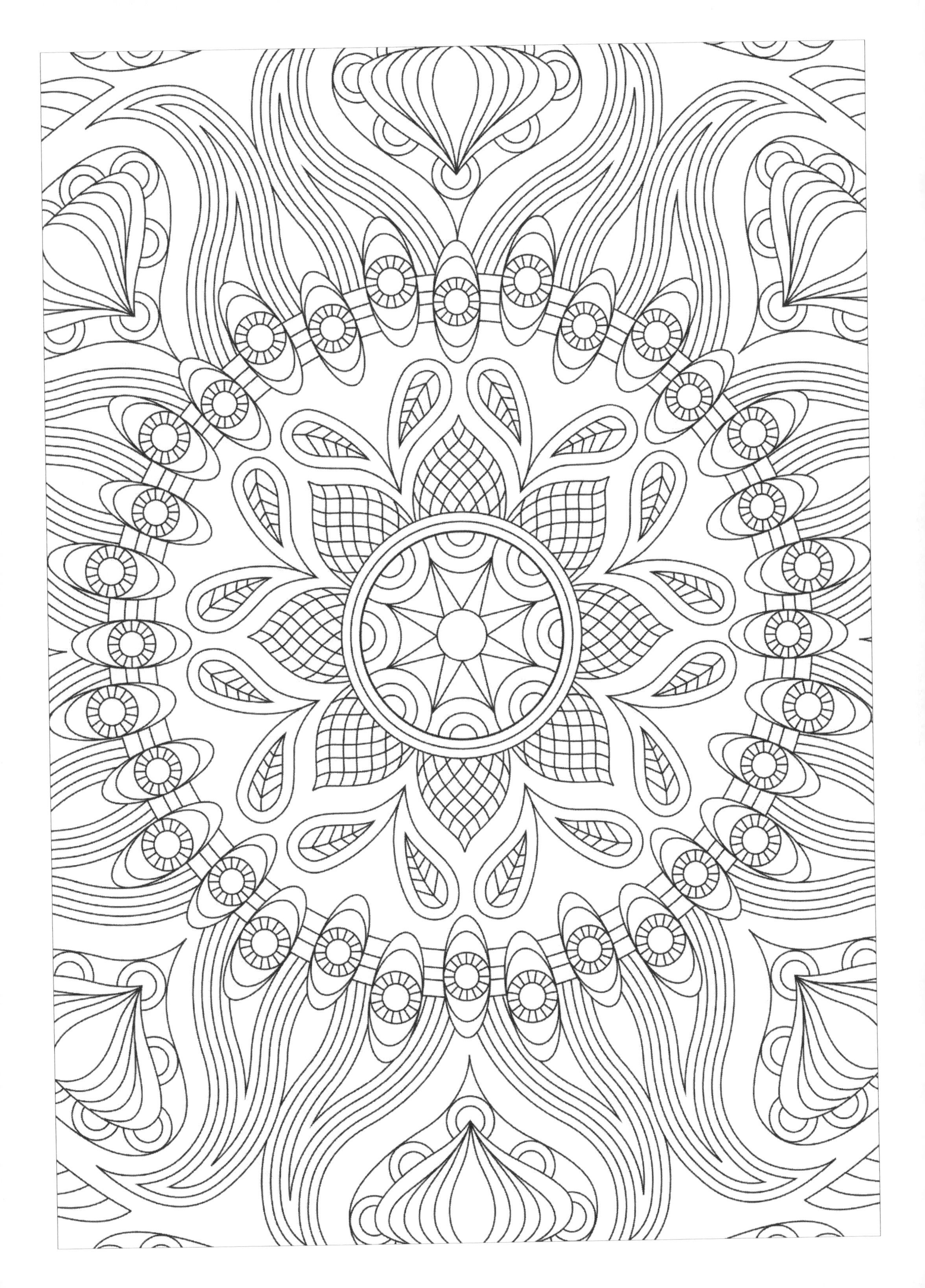

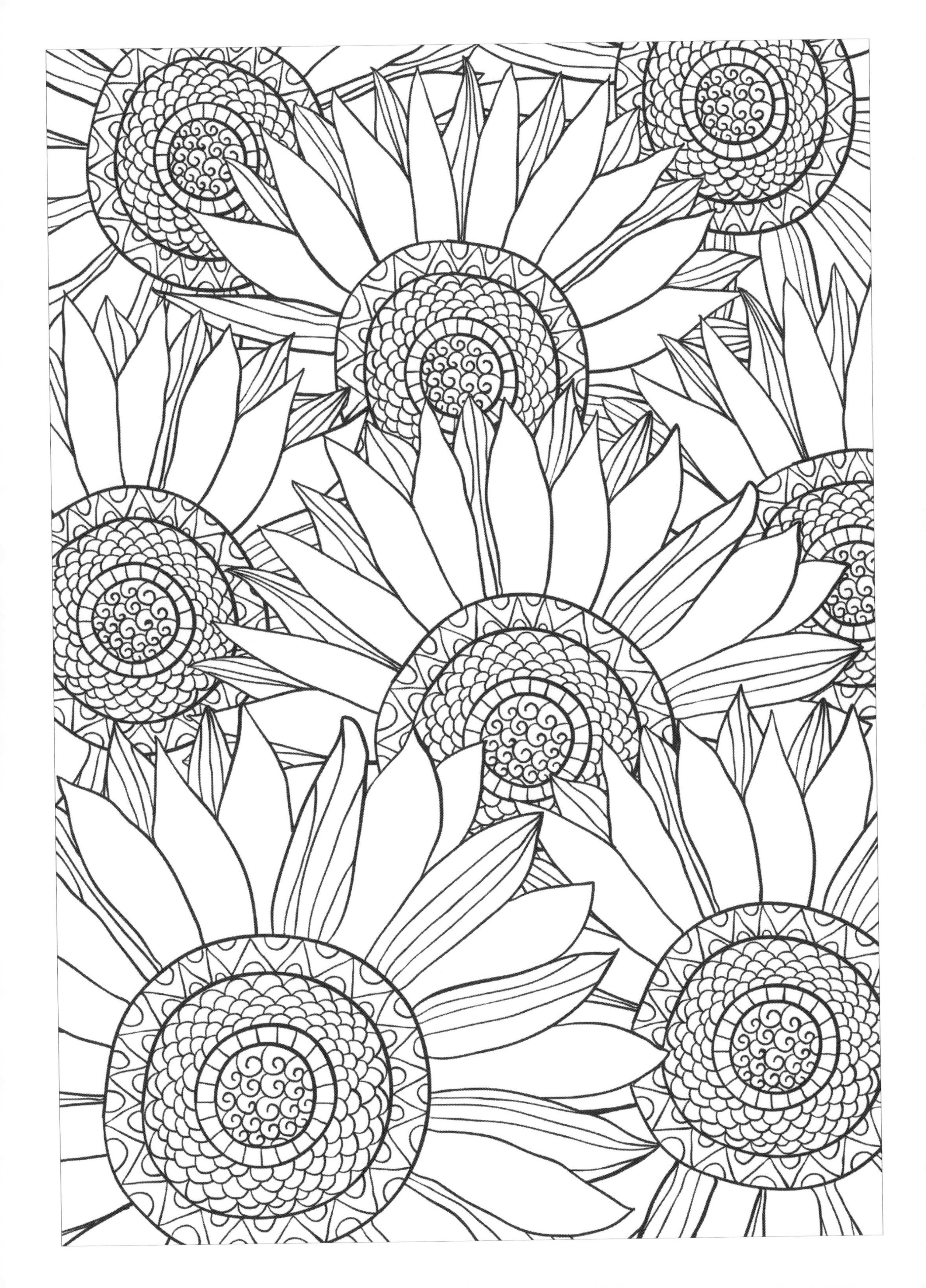

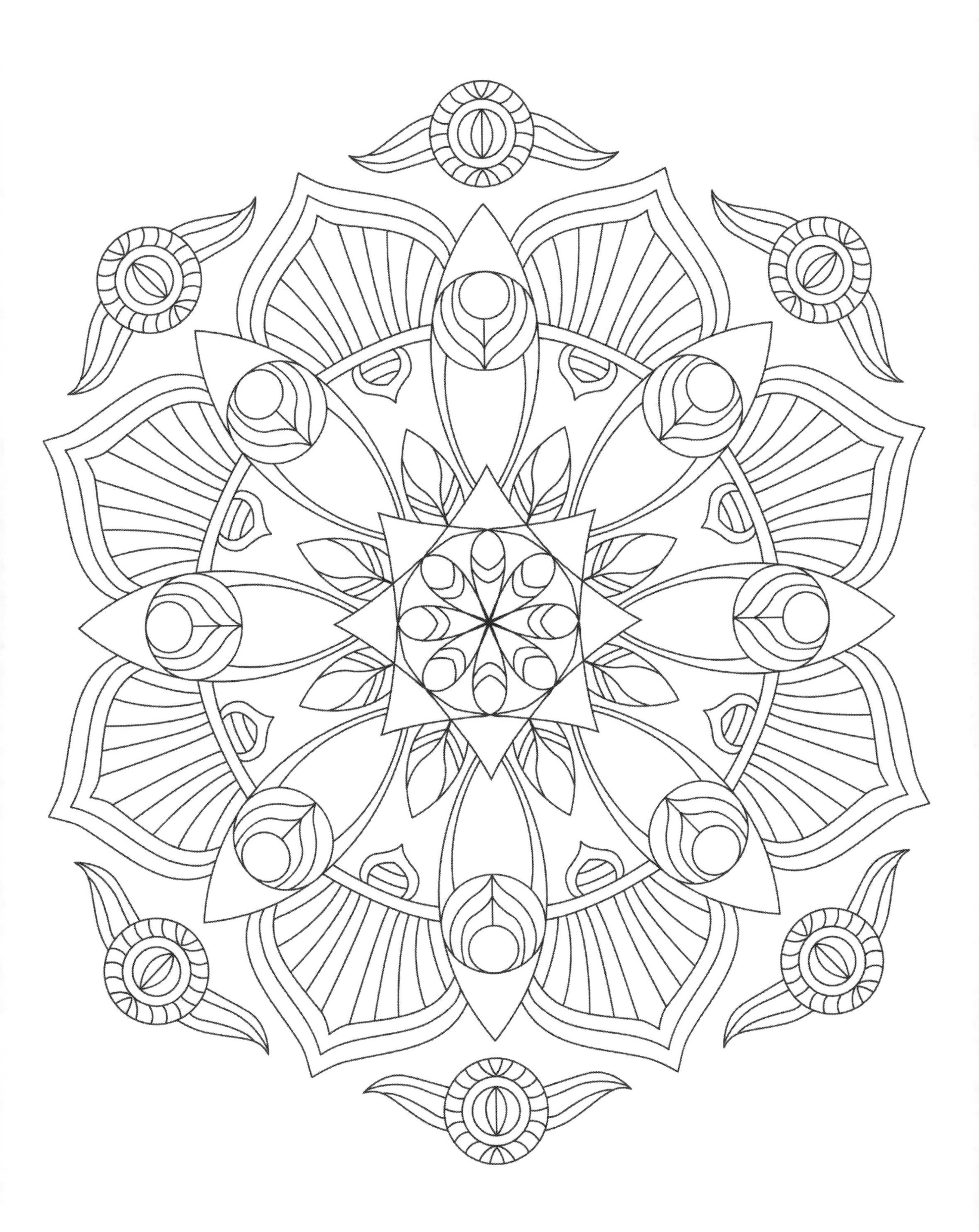

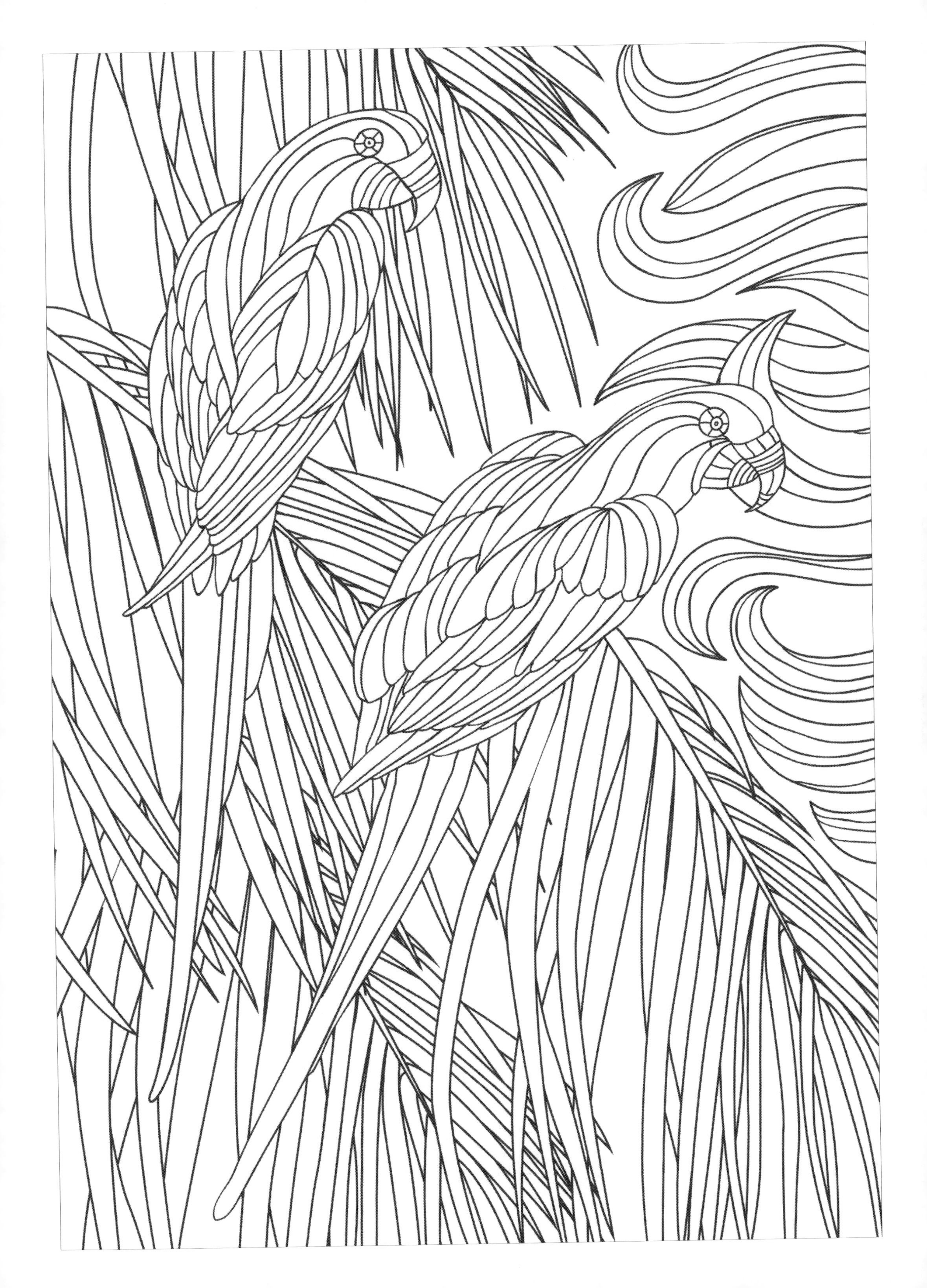

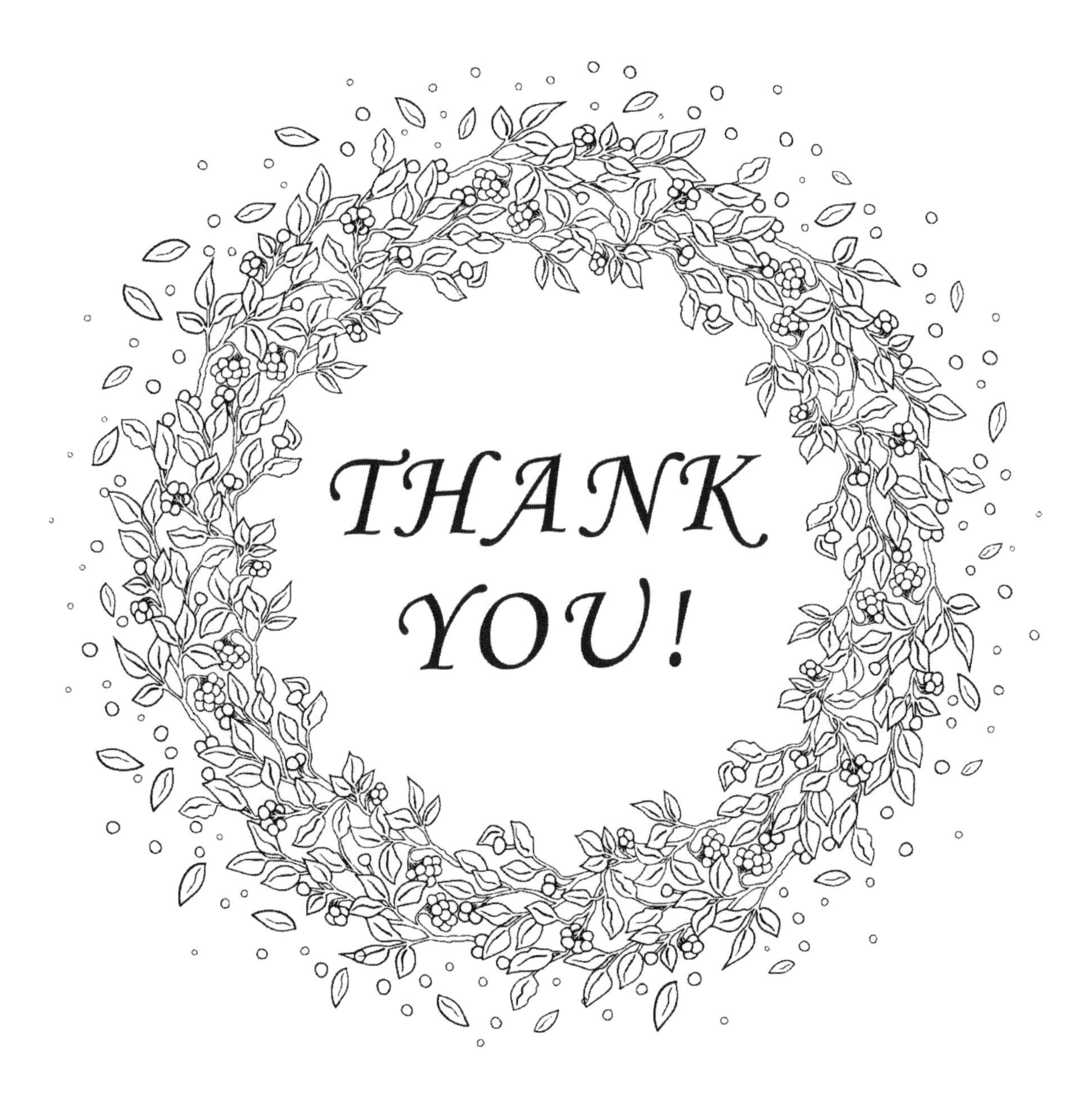

FROM THE AUTHOR

Thanks for coloring our book! I hope it was relaxing and I hope you had a lot of fun with it.

I would like to ask you for a *small* favor. Book reviews are very important for other coloring enthusiasts like you. If you have a minute, please leave a comment under our book here: www.coloringcraze.com/**review4**

It will help the buyers to make a decision and your feedback will be priceless to our illustrators ☺

All our other books are available here: www.coloringcraze.com/**our-books**

Remember to grab your **Free Bonus!**

=> http://www.coloringcraze.com/**bonus** <=

Thank You!

Printed in Great Britain
by Amazon